THE CHESHIRE RING IN CIRCULAR WALKS

Volume 1

Sally Bailey

SIGMA Leisure

Published by Sigma Leisure - an imprint of Sigma Press, Stobart House, Pontyclerc, Penybanc Road, Ammanford, Carmarthenshire SA18 3HP.

British Library Cataloguing in Publication Data
A CIP record for this book is available from the British Library.

ISBN: 978-1-85058-999-0

Typesetting and Design by: Sigma Press, Ammanford.

Cover photographs: top: Canal bridge at Lymm; below: Canal at bridge 94 of The Hall Green Branch © Sally Bailey

Photographs: © Sally Bailey unless stated otherwise.

Maps: Sigma Press

Printed by: Akcent Media

PREFACE

This book is the first of two volumes of canal side walks which together take you round the whole 97 miles of The Cheshire Ring. It contains 23 circular walks ranging from four and a half to eight and a half miles in length and takes you down the western side of The Ring. You will be walking along the Bridgewater Canal and The Trent and Mersey Canal, from the former's junction with the Rochdale Canal in the Castlefield area of Manchester in the north, to the latter's junction with the Macclesfield Canal at Hall Green near Kidsgrove in the south.

When I was a young child, my father obtained a key from British Waterways which allowed him access to the mainly derelict (at the time) Gas Street Basin in Birmingham. This opened up another world to me and I have been interested in canals ever since. After my husband and I had completed most of the walks in our books on Cheshire, I decided I wanted to walk round the Cheshire Ring. We were unable to find a book which took you round the Ring in circular walks so with my interest in walking, maps and local history, I thought I would devise and write one myself. We did the first walk, which is now Walk 22, in deep snow. Indeed, it was so deep that a very short section of the towpath was closed and we had to return the next week to complete the walk. It was not an auspicious start! It is now over four years and many, many walks later.

The walks are named after the section of canal you walk along but the actual walk itself may start elsewhere along the route. They can be walked in any order as each one stands completely alone, but if you start with Walk 1 in Castlefield and continue in order finishing with Walk 23, the feeling of progress around The Ring may be more evident. Every walk covers a stretch of between 2 and 3¾ miles along the towpath and a 'return' section on a combination of paths, tracks and roads, depending on the location of the walk.

The Ring itself is to be walked in an anticlockwise direction. That means in this book Volume 1 you are walking from north to south along the canals. However, due to the shape of The Ring, at times you will be travelling from east to west or from west to east. The length of each walk is approximate, as are the shorter distances given in the instructions. The time taken to do them is perhaps even more approximate and will vary, depending on the people involved, the weather and the length of the stops that are made. The more serious walker or those wishing to complete the first half of The Ring more quickly, may even wish to combine two walks together to make a longer walk, as they follow on from each other.

Some of the walks, especially the shorter ones, might be suitable for children, but be aware of the dangers presented by the canals and by busy roads. If you plan to go with children, I suggested that you read through the walk carefully before making your decision. On the whole the stiles and paths are in good condition, none of the walks are strenuous, and generally the most strenuous part of any walk is the climbing of stiles and navigating muddy fields after rain. It might be sensible to wear walking boots especially in rural areas, unless advised otherwise. Remember as in all walks, care should be taken by everyone at all times.

Every walk contains a map and some photographs. At the end of the walk there is information on some of the places and features which might be of interest, plus details of pubs and cafés nearby. I have only commented on those we have visited, and any lack of comment does not mean they are not worthy, but simply that I have not been there. Phone numbers and where available, websites, are given and it is suggested that if in doubt places are contacted before going, as opening hours can easily change. Unfortunately establishments can also suddenly close as we have found to our dismay. Having discovered a pub in Wheelock which produced the most wonderful chocolate pudding, we went again to find that it had become an ethnic restaurant!

At the end of the book is a log which can be filled in to show your progress round The Ring. There is also a place for comments and anything else you may wish to record.

It is hoped that the walks give as much pleasure to other walkers as they have given to me.

The author can take no responsibility if for any reason the towpath or any footpath is closed, and strongly suggests you always take the relevant Ordnance Survey map with you in the unlikely event that your walk needs re-routing. Nor can she take any responsibility if any of the information given in the directions or in any other part of the book is incorrect, as it was all correct at the time of writing.

I would like to dedicate this book to my mother Gladys Royle

Who else?

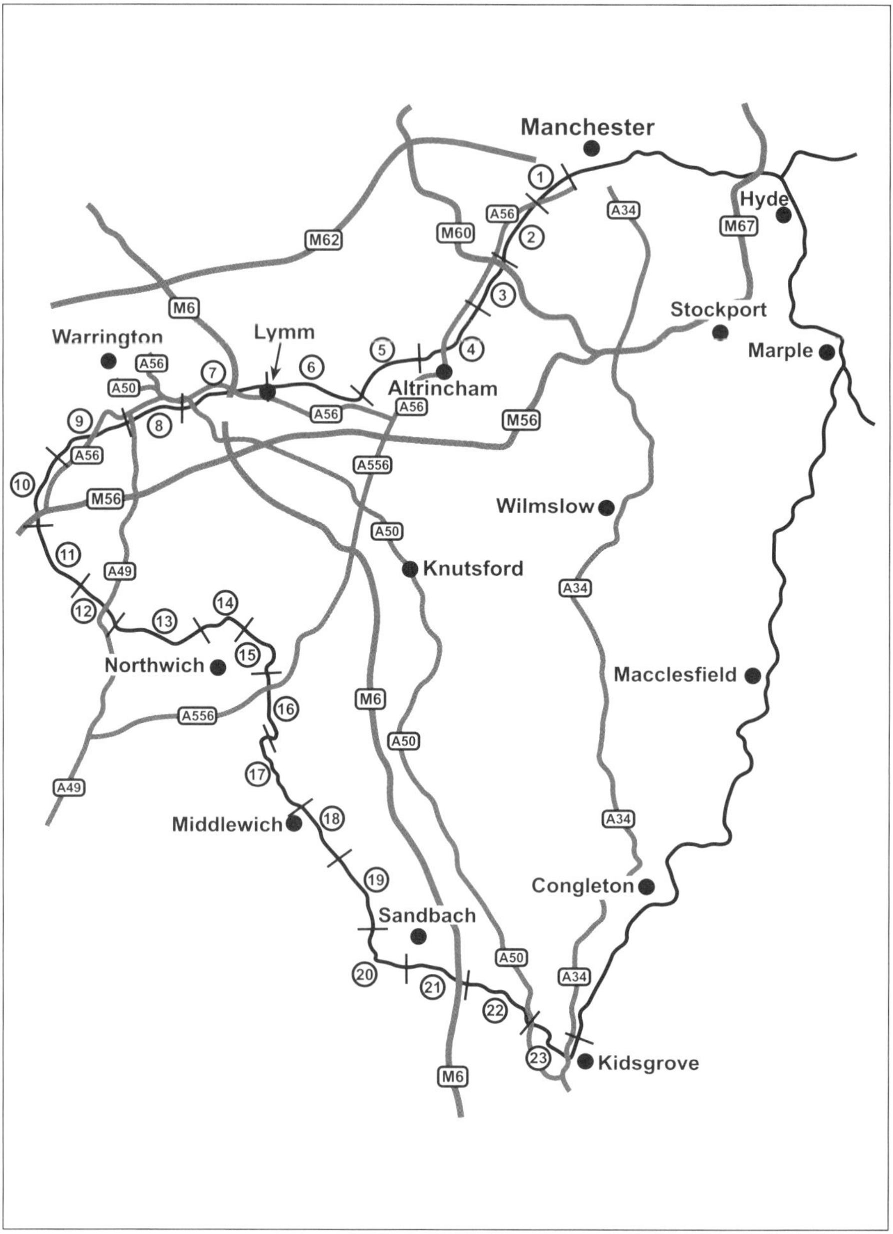

Locations of walks

CONTENTS

Introduction			9
1.	Castlefield to Old Trafford	4½ to 5 miles	17
2.	Old Trafford to Stretford	5½ miles	29
3.	Stretford to Brooklands	6½ miles	36
4.	Brooklands to Seamons Moss	6 miles	44
5.	Seamons Moss to Little Bollington	4½ to 5 miles	51
6.	Little Bollington to Lymm	7 miles	58
7.	Lymm to Grappenhall	6½miles	66
8.	Grappenhall to Stockton Heath	4½ to 5 miles	71
9.	Stockton Heath to Moore	7 miles	78
10.	Moore to Preston Brook	6½ to 7 miles	85
11.	Preston Brook to Lodge Lane	5½ miles	93
12.	Lodge Lane to south of Acton Bridge	5 miles	100
13.	South of Acton Bridge to Anderton	6½ miles	106
14.	Anderton to Marston	4½ miles	113
15.	Marston to Rudheath	4½ miles	120
16.	Rudheath to Whatcroft	5 to 5½ miles	126
17.	Whatcroft to The Big Lock, Middlewich	8½ miles	131
18.	The Big Lock, Middlewich to Tetton Bridge	6 miles	138
19.	Tetton Bridge to Elworth	5 miles	146
20.	Elworth to Wheelock	6½ miles	151
21.	Wheelock to Hassall Green	5 miles	157
22.	Hassall Green to Rode Heath	5 miles	163
23.	Rode Heath to Hall Green via Hardings Wood Junction	5½ to 6 miles	168

Acknowledgements

I would like to thank my husband Don Bailey who has come on every walk with me at least twice and in many cases, three times. He also read my first drafts and helped me make the necessary corrections before we embarked on the walks for the second time. However, his volunteering to test out the pubs as we went along was perhaps not quite such a chore!

In addition I want to thank all my friends and family who have tried out the walks and have given me help and encouragement over the past couple of years, especially Jenni Mills for her practical advice. Extra special thanks must go to my sister Sue Cowley not only for the many hours she spent proof reading and helping me modify my final drafts but also for her constant encouragement and support.

Finally I would like to thank my publishers Sigma Leisure who have eased me gently through the process of getting this book published and who have made the whole task less daunting than it might otherwise have been.

INTRODUCTION

The Cheshire Ring is 97 miles of navigable inland waterways. Its circular route through Cheshire links Castlefield, Manchester in the north with Hardings Wood Junction near Kidsgrove in the south and Northwich and Middlewich in the west with Congleton and Macclesfield in the east. Travelling southwards in an anticlockwise direction from Castlefield, it crosses The Cheshire Plain then rises as it turns back northwards across the foothills of The Pennines, before descending again to Manchester. In the whole Ring there are 250 bridges, 83 locks and 5 tunnels - Preston Brook, Saltersford, Barnton, Hyde Bank and Woodley Tunnels. This book, Volume 1, takes you down the western side of The Cheshire Ring, along the Bridgewater and Trent and Mersey Canals, in 23 circular walks.

The name 'The Cheshire Ring' was first used in the mid 1960s by The Peak Forest Canal Society whose aim was to get the Lower Peak Forest Canal, including the Marple Locks, restored. In order to obtain publicity for its cause, the Society wanted to promote the idea of a ring of canals around Cheshire which could be used by pleasure craft once all the canals had been restored to working order. However, the Lower Peak Forest Canal was not the only part of the Ring that was derelict, as the Ashton Canal and Rochdale Canal were perhaps in an even worse state of repair. There were numerous setbacks and many battles not only with The British Waterways Board but also with local authorities. Eventually thanks to the persistence of a number of far sighted people, and the tireless work of many volunteers, The Cheshire Ring was finally opened in 1974.

Castlefield, Manchester

Castlefield, Manchester is the starting point for walk no. 1, the first of the 23 circular walks in this book, Volume 1. The final walk in Volume 2 will end back again in Castlefield, to complete The Ring.

In 1765 Castlefield became the northern terminus of the Bridgewater Canal. Its construction enabled coal to be brought from Worsley to the city centre, and according to some, this was the true start of the Industrial Revolution. A number of basins and canal arms were built and warehouses were erected. When the Rochdale Canal joined The Bridgewater Canal here in 1800, the area became an even more important transport hub, although the route across the Pennines was not completed until 1804.

The growth of the railways from the 1830s onwards, resulted in the slow decline of the canals for both goods and passenger transport. Interestingly it was on nearby Liverpool Road that Britain's first rail passenger station was built. The railway lines in the vicinity were soon used to transport goods faster and at a more competitive price than the canals and by the mid 20th century much of the area around the canals in Castlefield was run down or derelict. However, in 1982 Castlefield became the United Kingdom's first Urban Heritage Park, and it was after this that its 'rebirth' began.

Two years later Peel Holdings purchased The Bridgewater Estates, and the 1988 Inland Waterways Rally in Castlefield was a huge impetus for its regeneration. The canals were dredged, the area tidied up and it is now a vibrant residential, small business and commercial community, having changed beyond all recognition. The suspended curved walkway of Merchants Bridge which spans the start of The Bridgewater Canal marks a fitting beginning and end to the walks around The Cheshire Ring.

The Bridgewater Canal

The Bridgewater Canal forms the north western section of The Cheshire Ring. The stretch of the canal which forms part of The Ring runs for 23 miles from Castlefield in Manchester to Preston Brook. It is connected to the Rochdale

Original start of the Bridgewater Canal, Castlefield, cut into rock

Canal and Manchester Ship Canal in Manchester, The Trent and Mersey Canal at Preston Brook, and the Liverpool and Leigh Canal at Leigh on the Leigh Branch of the canal. The Bridgewater Canal is a deep, broad waterway, and apart from Pomona Locks leading to the Manchester Ship Canal, it contains no locks. From Castlefield, the canal winds its way through suburban south Manchester which is greener than one might think then leaves the conurbation to flow through countryside punctuated by mainly small settlements before joining the Trent and Mersey Canal on the south side of Preston Brook.

The Bridgewater Canal was the first 'industrial age' canal and the first canal in Britain to be built as a completely independent water course. Its construction was totally down to the vision of one man - Francis Egerton, the Third Duke of Bridgewater whose father the first duke, owned mines in Worsley. However from the beginning there were problems getting the coal to its markets because the only means of transporting it was by packhorse on unreliable roads which made the journey very difficult and costly. In 1757, Francis returned to Worsley to take charge of the vast estate, including the mines. As a young man he had travelled on The Grand Tour of Europe and using the knowledge he had gained abroad, especially from seeing the Grand Lauguedoc Canal in France (later known as the Canal du Midi) he decided to have a canal constructed to transport the coal. He employed John Gilbert as a mine agent and engineer, and Gilbert, in turn introduced the Duke to James Brindley.

James Brindley had a fundamental understanding of what was needed to build a waterway. Even though he later built a number of other canals, his reputation was made by the construction of the Bridgewater Canal and in particular The Barton Aqueduct. Although this is on the Leigh Branch of the canal and not part of the Cheshire Ring, its construction was vital for the success of the canal.

In 1761 The Bridgewater Canal was opened from Worsley (now on the Leigh Branch) to Stretford. On the canal's opening day, the price of coal in Manchester halved. Four years later the canal was extended to Castlefield which became its terminus. Meanwhile, in 1763 the first connection, known as The Gut, was made to The Mersey and Irwell Navigation at Cornbrook. Soon after this, work was started to extend the canal to Preston Brook, and work also began on the Runcorn Branch of the canal. In 1768 the canal reached Lymm, in the following year it was opened as far as Stockton Heath, and in 1772 it was finally extended to Preston Brook. In the same year, 1772, Brindley died, Gilbert died in 1795, and the well-liked duke, died in 1803. However he was alive to see the opening of the Rochdale Canal, to join with The Bridgewater Canal at Castlefield in 1800.

In 1826, The Liverpool and Manchester Railway Act was passed, and the railway age had arrived. In order to compete with the railways, new warehouses and loading facilities were constructed at Castlefield and Preston Brook, so that cargo could be moved more quickly to and from the boats. In 1838 Hulme Locks were built to replace The Gut. Even though the railways did not immediately damage the canal's fortunes, the Bridgwater Canal Company needed to remain competitive, so in 1846 they bought The Manchester and Irwell Navigation for £550,000 and formed The Bridgewater Navigation Company. This in turn was bought in 1885 by the newly formed Manchester Ship Canal Company, who then became the owners of the canal.

Although the canal had been built to transport coal and subsequently other goods, and this was its primary function, it was also used as a means of passenger transport. As early as 1767, packet boats had started to carry passengers. This business grew over time and by the mid 19th century passenger boats were in regular service on the canal. Stockton Heath was one of the major stopping off points and the circular boat steps can still be seen here. In 1851 Queen Victoria took a trip from Patricroft to Worsley (on the Leigh Branch) and in 1869 The Prince of Wales travelled on the canal from Worsley to Trafford.

Eventually steam tugs replaced the use of horses to pull the boats and these continued to be used until the 1920s, when some were converted to diesel and the rest were sold or scrapped. As the 20th century progressed, trade gradually fell. In 1952 it was decided to encourage the canal's use for pleasure craft and a number of boating clubs opened along the canal. These include The Watch House in Stretford and boating clubs in Sale, Lymm and Preston Brook. Commercial traffic finally ceased in 1974 although the occasional narrow boat can be seen taking coal to boats still using solid fuel.

The Bridgewater Canal is now owned and operated by The Manchester Ship Canal Company, part of Peel Holdings. This is conjunction with the Bridgewater Canal Trust which was set up after a huge canal breach near Dunham Massey in 1971. They also own the towpath, and in recent years have done much work to upgrade it. In 2011 a resurfaced section between Waters Meeting and Sale was opened, some of which is part of a new Sustrans Cycle route. The Bridgewater Way Regeneration Project eventually hopes to create an upgraded leisure route along the whole length of The Bridgewater Canal, and so make it an even more attractive environment for walkers.

The Trent and Mersey Canal

The Trent and Mersey Canal forms the south western section of the Cheshire Ring. The whole canal is 93 miles long and runs from its junction with the

Bridgewater Canal just south of Preston Brook to its junction with the River Trent at Derwent Mouth. The section of the canal which forms part of The Cheshire Ring runs for 30 miles from Preston Brook to Hardings Wood Junction, with an additional 1¼ mile spur to Hall Green to join the Macclesfield Canal. There are also connections with The Shropshire Union Canal in Middlewich and The River Weaver via The Anderton Boat Lift. Its route through The Cheshire Plain is largely rural, apart from the sections through Northwich and Middlewich. However, both towns hold some pleasant surprises, including the Northwich flashes and the area round the locks in Middlewich. A number of small canal side communities are also passed.

Unlike the Bridgewater Canal, whose only lock is to connect it to The Manchester Ship Canal, the Trent and Mersey has two flights of locks: The Middlewich Locks, numbers 75 to 67, from Big Lock up to Crows Nest Lock and just to the south of this, The Cheshire Locks which take you from lock 66 near Wheelock, up to Lock 41 at Hardings Wood Junction. These 26 Cheshire Locks known to canal users over the years as 'Heartbreak Hill' take the walker from the flat Cheshire Plain to part way up the foothills of the Pennines. All but two were rebuilt by Telford as paired locks, and even though they do not all remain in their original form, they are a delight to see and a pleasure to walk past. Other notable features on The Trent and Mersey Canal include the cast iron mileposts which for some reason measure the mileage to Shardlow and not Derwent Mouth. Of the 93 mileposts, 59 of the original ones made in the Rougeley and Dixon foundry still remain, and 34 have been replaced. The replacements bear the mark of the Trent and Mersey Canal Society.

The Trent and Mersey Canal was conceived with the idea of linking the ports of Hull and Liverpool. Like The Duke of Bridgewater, Josiah Wedgewood saw the huge benefits of carrying goods by water rather than on the slow, difficult and costly roads. He realised that the quicker, cheaper and safer carriage of goods offered by canals, would benefit both his and other industries. After gaining much interest in, and support for the project, he appointed James Brindley as chief engineer who unfortunately then died soon after from a chill he contracted whilst surveying the route. The whole 93 mile long canal was finally opened in 1777. It connected The Potteries to mid Cheshire, and more importantly to The River Mersey and the port of Liverpool via The Bridgewater Canal. The River Weaver could also be accessed using The Anderton Boat Lift.

As soon as it opened, The Trent and Mersey Canal was a great success. Large quantities of china clay and flints were brought by sea from the South West to Liverpool, from where they were taken to Runcorn via the River Mersey. Here they were transhipped into canal boats and transported along the canals to factories in the Stoke area. Coal was also brought in by canal to fuel the

Looking down from Poole Aqueduct towards Hardings Wood Junction

new industries. Salt travelled in the opposite direction from the Northwich and Middlewich areas via the canal system to Liverpool. Indeed it is said that over 10 million tons of combined rock salt and white salt was exported between 1880 and 1890. Many other commodities were transported by the canal including Cheshire cheese. Industry grew and so created jobs, lower freight charges meant cheaper goods and many people benefitted from the canal. Even agriculture benefitted as a new water supply was created.

In 1845 the Trent and Mersey Canal was taken over by the newly created Staffordshire Railway Company. Note the awnings reminiscent of the railways over the covered dock near Preston Brook Tunnel. The canal continued to successfully carry freight until well into the 20th century as it was an important trading route. Nowadays although there is no longer any commercial traffic on the Trent and Mersey Canal, it is a very popular pleasure cruising waterway.

In 2012 the British Waterways Board was disbanded and the management of the canals was taken over by a charity, The Canal and River Trust (**www.canalrivertrust.org**). Its ability to deal with big and expensive issues was tested almost at once with the breaches at Croxton Aqueduct (Walk 16) and on a larger scale Dutton (Walk 12) in September 2012. From the results, it appears they are doing an excellent job.

The Salt Industry of Cheshire

The area of Cheshire around and to the south of Northwich has been exploited for its salt since Roman times. After the Romans left, interest in salt extraction waned but the salt beds were re-discovered in 1670 by John Jackson who, when looking for coal in the grounds of Marbury Hall, found rock salt instead. By the late 19th century it became uneconomical to go underground to mine salt, so a new way to extract it had to be found. In the end it was discovered that if hot water was pumped through the mines, the salt would dissolve. The brine could then be pumped out and the salt extracted from that. Unfortunately this process had a disastrous effect on any area where it took place as it led to much local subsidence. This was widespread but the problem has been most evident in and around Northwich.

From walk 13 onwards you will see evidence of the years of salt extraction in various forms including: the salt towns of Northwich and Middlewich ('wich' means salt); the many flashes including the large Neumann's Flashes, Ashton's Flashes and Watch Lane Flash; the 'wides' south of Northwich; the subsidence around the village of Marston and 'The Salt Line' on Walk 22. You will pass British Salt and other associated industries including the two huge Tata Chemical complexes near Northwich and the former Brunner Mond sites. You will also see the dereliction left from the lime beds which were created as a result of the salt industry, although much of this land has now been reclaimed.

Each of the walks in this book is in two distinct parts. There is a stretch of canal which is generally between 2 and 3 miles in length plus a section that takes you back to where you began on the canal. The actual start of the walk can be at any point on the route, but where possible it is where you join the canal, following on from the previously numbered walk. The walks therefore not only take you half way round The Ring, they also bring you back through very varied and interesting scenery, both rural and urban, and hold many surprises and joys. Along the canals there are the obvious highlights of The Anderton Boat Lift; the two flights of locks, especially the paired locks of 'Heartbreak Hill', and the interesting villages of Lymm, Grappenhall, Moore, Anderton, Malkin's Bank and Rode Heath. However, perhaps the greatest pleasure along the canals can be gained from the unexpected finds. These include; bluebells and lily of the valley in the spring around the Acton Bridge area; the 'wides' just south of Northwich; the many meandering rural stretches of waterway, and the views looking eastwards from the locks ascending towards the Pennines. Off the canals there are also the more obvious highlight such as Salford Quays; Dunham Massey Hall, Park and Gardens and the main Lion Salt Works complex. Yet again, it is the unexpected finds that perhaps bring even more pleasure.

These include numerous small copses and woods, often with meandering streams and bluebells in the spring; some wonderful field paths with magnificent view; reclaimed flashes such as Neumanns Flashes and Watch Lane Flash which are now havens for wildfowl, and former salt workings and other industrial areas which have been made into attractive nature parks. Greater Manchester also contains some 'rural' surprises including Longford Park and Gardens, Sale Water Park, Sale Ees, Chorlton Ees, and paths along lesser brooks, so well hidden that even if you know the area you may not be aware of them.

'Cheshire Ring' canal sign at Hardings Wood Junction

There are many places to stop for refreshment both on the canal side and close by and these are listed at the end of each walk. Amongst those worth mentioning are The Broughton Arms (walk 22) and the Red Bull (walk 23) which have pleasant sitting out areas overlooking the canal and the dog friendly Swan with Two Nicks (walks 5 and 6), although there are many more to choose from. Yet perhaps the most welcome finds are the serendipitous ones especially when you are in need of sustenance and they seem to appear just at the right time, as happened on a number of occasions to the author. These include Riverside Organics Café south of Northwich (walk 16) which we came to, seemingly in the middle of nowhere, at the start of a heavy shower and The London Arms Pub in Stockton Heath (walks 8 and 9) which opened its doors and offered hot drinks to a group of cold walkers one New Years Day morning. However if you want a walk where most of your time could be spent indulging, you cannot beat walk 5 where you pass 2 pubs, 2 cafés and a micro-brewery in less than 5 miles!

Cheshire is a county of many contrasts. When all the walks in this book have eventually been completed you will not only have the satisfaction and sense of achievement of knowing you have walked half of the Cheshire Ring, but also, in the process, you will have been taken through parts of hidden Cheshire you perhaps never knew existed.

WALK 1
Castlefield to Old Trafford

Castlefield – The Bridgewater Canal – Old Trafford – Salford Quays – Ordsall – The Manchester Ship Canal – The River Irwell - Castlefield

Starting point	**Merchants Bridge, Castlefield. Grid reference: 831975**
Length	**4½-5 miles**
Allow	**Approximately 2 hours**
Map	**OS Explorer 277**
By car	**Park towards the south of Deansgate or near Castlefield. Make your way to Merchants Bridge in the centre of Castlefield**
By Metrolink	**Take the Manchester Metrolink to Deansgate/Castlefield (formerly G-Mex). Descend the steps, cross Deansgate, and follow the signs ahead, to walk down the cobbled street to the left of the canal bridge. This leads round to the right to reach the centre of Castlefield and Merchants Bridge**

If this is the first of your walks around the Cheshire Ring, although not representative of what is to come, it is a fitting start. The canals were initially built to serve industry and industrial growth, and on this walk you can clearly see the contrast between the old and the new. Indeed, this section of the Bridgewater Canal, constructed to bring coal to Manchester from The Duke of Bridgewater's mines in Worsley, was part of the first true canal to be built in the country. It heralded the start of the 'canal revolution'.

It is a very varied walk, passing well designed modern apartments and large visionary developments, which contrast with semi industrial areas. In addition to The Bridgewater Canal, you also walk along the old redeveloped Salford Docks (now Salford Quays), the Manchester Ship Canal and the River Irwell. You also pass The Imperial War Museum North, The Lowry Centre with Media City behind it and the Museum of Science and Industry which is on the site of first railway station in Britain. This walk sets the scene and introduces you to the Bridgewater Canal and to contrasting canal side developments both past and present. Enjoy it in the knowledge that it leads on to more!

The Walk

1. Begin the walk in the centre of *Castlefield* at the south Western corner of Merchants Bridge. You cannot miss the elegant, sweep-ing bridge, a worthy start to a walk round the Cheshire Ring. Come off the bridge at the end furthest from the main bars/ cafés and railway arches. Turn sharp left and left again. This is the start of The Bridgewater Canal. The Rochdale Canal is behind you. You will have the water to your right for almost 1½ miles before leaving the towpath just after bridge 95 and shortly before reaching Old Trafford Football Stadium.

Merchants Bridge, Castlefield

2. Walk in a westerly direction away from the bridge, leaving Castlefield behind. Pass the cobbled Slate Wharf with apartments to your left. After walking over two small bridges you will see an old flour mill on your left. Note the tower, the design of which came from Northern Italy. About 250 yards after Merchants Bridge, walk under the A57(M) road bridge.

The start of the Bridgewater Canal, Castlefield

3. Once under the bridge you will see a large building on your left. This was once an arms manufactory and weapons store run by Samuel Cummins. It has now been converted into apartments and is one of a number of buildings in the area which have been redeveloped by Urban Splash. Opposite are Hulme Locks which once led to

The River Irwell and the Manchester Ship Canal, but they are no longer in use. Pass more apartments on your left, and the St Georges Island Apartments on your right. Cross a bridge over a small inlet.

4. Continue under Hulme Hall Bridge, go over a ramp and past more apartments on your left. Walk under a bridge carrying the metro line and the landscape changes. You have now left the apartments and fashionable inner city behind, and until you leave the towpath, the canal meanders through what is at present a relatively empty landscape. Beyond this to your right is The Manchester Ship Canal. Pass Cornbrook station up to your left.

5. Shortly afterwards you will see *Pomona Locks* (built to replace Hulme Locks) on your right, which give access to The Manchester Ship Canal. Immediately after Pomona Locks, walk under the metro line again and note Pomona Station on your right, which is on the line to Eccles. Take care along this section as the towpath is relatively narrow. Cross over the canal on the attractive Throstle Nest footbridge, and once over, turn right to join the towpath, now on the opposite side of the canal.

Throstle Nest Footbridge

6. Continue in the same direction, this time with the water on your left and go under two wide road bridges in quick succession. Straight after the second bridge and just before a large brick warehouse you will see some steps to the right. Go up this path beside the warehouse.

7. At the top, turn left and cross Trafford Wharf Road at the pedestrian traffic lights which are on your right. Continue forward towards the Manchester Ship Canal, noting the Trafford Park sign and anchor sculpture on your left. Cross Wharf End to reach the canal bank. Turn left just before the bridge over the Ship Canal.

8. Walk along the pavement with the metro line and Manchester Ship Canal to your right until you come to Wharfside Metrolink Station. Go through

the station to cross the rail line then turn left onto the walkway alongside the Ship Canal. Walk along here with the metro line now to your left for about ⅓ mile until you reach *The Lowry Bridge.*

The raised Lowry Bridge with The Lowry Centre and Media city behind

9. There continues to be redevelopment in this area, and many interesting new buildings can be seen on either side of the canal. This is a pleasant section of the walk, and there are good views of *Salford Quays, the Lowry Centre,* Media City and *the Lowry Bridge* which links the Imperial War Museum North with the Lowry Centre.

10. If you wish to visit the *Imperial War Museum North,* which is well worth seeing, go past the *Lowry Bridge* and follow the signs. Granada Studios and the set of Coronation Street is also just along here on the left. To continue the walk, when you reach the bridge, turn right to cross over the Ship Canal. Note, just before the bridge, there is an information board telling you about walking trails in the area. In the unlikely event the bridge is raised, simply walk on, cross another bridge and walk back to The Lowry via Media City.

11. Once over *The Lowry Bridge* you may wish to visit *The Lowry Centre* which is to your left. However, to continue the walk, come off the bridge, turn right and walk along the wide walkway for about ¼ mile with Central Bay to your right. This side of the canal is just as pleasant as the one you have just walked along, and you will pass between two rows of trees.

12. When you reach a watersports centre on your left, turn right to pass Salford Quays Operations Tower and cross the narrow bridge over Ontario Basin. Once over the basin, keep to the left of The Holiday Inn, and continuing to keep left, walk alongside the basin, with the water now on your left. After just under 200 yards, when you reach the small Chandlers Canal, turn to your right, go up some steps and turn left to cross the small canal. Continue along the road, in the same direction.

Ontario Basin and walkway, Salford Quays

13. After about 100 yards you come to the metro line and a main road. Cross here at the traffic lights, taking extreme care because the traffic coming from your right is turning towards you from the road opposite, so you must look to see what is coming from the road ahead. Continue in the same direction and you will very soon reach some more traffic lights. Here you cross the main Trafford Road then turn left. After about 50 yards and just before reaching Ordsall Park, turn right past black bollards onto a wide footpath.

14. Walk along the footpath which soon becomes a road, and just before it bears right as Craven Drive, turn left into the park. Take the path to your immediate right so you are walking towards a large block of flats at the far end of the park. Note the small information plaques which help visitors identify some of the things they might see. Walk parallel to the right hand side of the park, cross another path, ignore the next paths that come from your right and left then take the next right which is almost at the far corner of the park with street lights along it. It is just over 250 yards after entering the park and just before you reach the block of flats. Once out of the park,

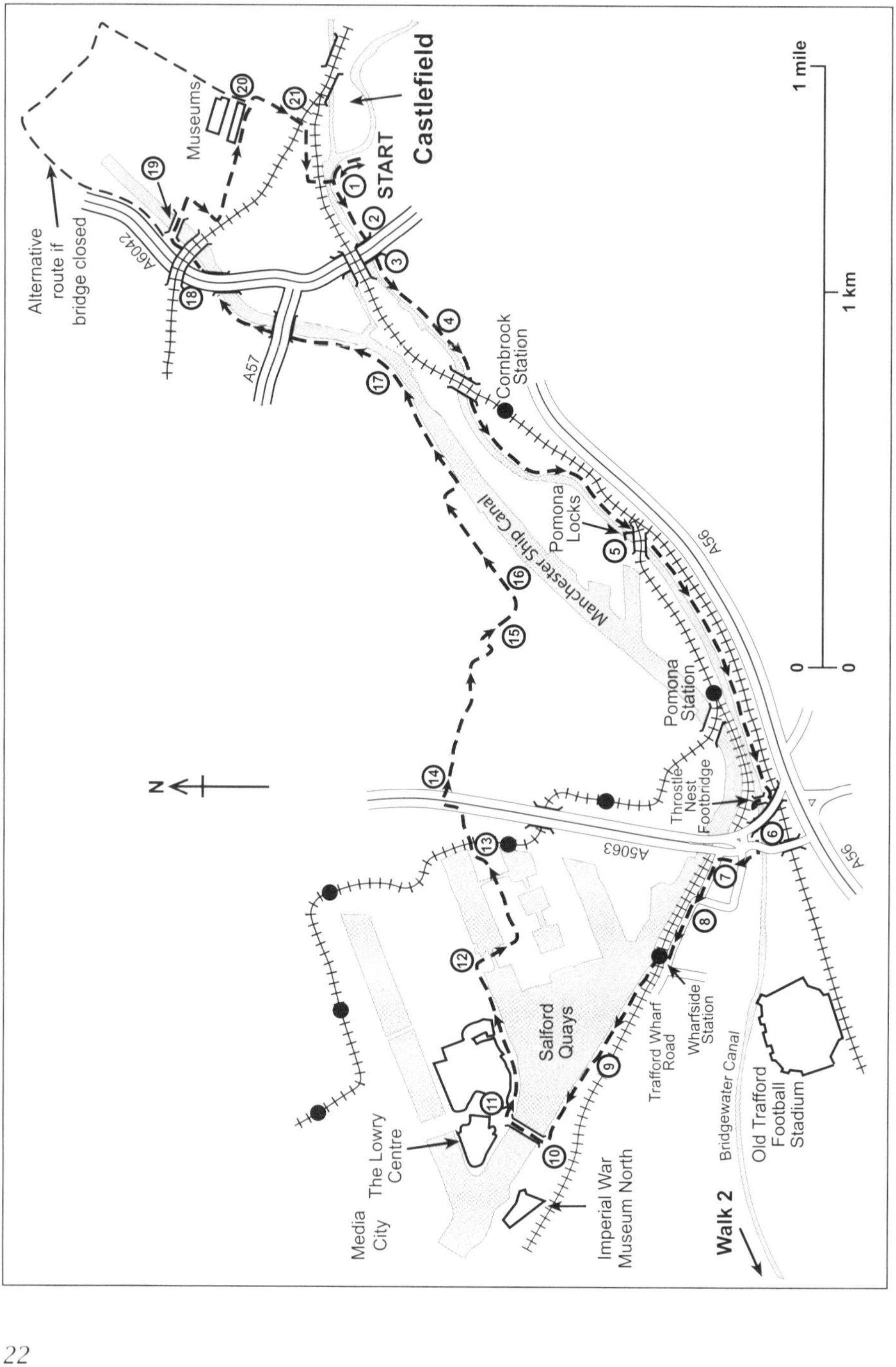
Castlefield
START
Museums
Alternative route if bridge closed
A6042
A57
Cornbrock Station
Pomona Locks
Manchester Ship Canal
A56
Pomona Station
Throstle Nest Footbridge
A5063
N
Salford Quays
Wharfside Station
Trafford Wharf Road
Bridgewater Canal
Old Trafford Football Stadium
The Lowry Centre
Media City
Imperial War Museum North
Walk 2

turn left and almost immediately left again into Taylorson Street. Just before the tall block of flats, take a path to your right between the flats and houses. This leads you down Nine Acres Drive.

15. When you reach Ordsall Lane, turn left and after about 150 yards turn right into Fairbrother Street, which will lead you to the canal in 150 yards. If for any reason the canal towpath is closed here, as has occurred in the past, continue along Ordsall Lane until you reach The Bricklayers Arms on your left, then turn right along Woden Street. At the end of here you can join the canal.

16. When the path reaches the ship canal turn left along a well designed walkway. Nowadays the water here appears to be clean enough for swans to feel it is worth diving for food! Note the interesting graffiti and murals along this stretch. After almost ¼ mile, walk under a footbridge. It is at this point, The Manchester Ship Canal becomes The River Irwell, although you would not notice that this had occurred.

17. Pass the far side of the St Georges Island Apartments and at the end of the railway viaduct you can see the other end of the derelict Hulme Locks. Walk past the back of a new apartment development on the other side of the canal, and continue under the A57, Regent Road bridge. The river now bears to the right. When you are half way under the next road bridge, take the clear path that leads up ahead to your left to join the main road. If you reach the railway bridge you have gone too far.

18. Once on the road, turn right and pass under a railway bridge. If Princess Bridge to your right is open, go up and over it. Note, regeneration is taking place, so the following directions may need modification. When you reach Water Street, turn right, walk under two bridges then turn left onto Liverpool Road. Almost immediately pass the former *Liverpool Road Station*, the first passenger railway station in England, followed by the *Manchester Museum of Science and Industry*. Straight after this, turn right

19. If Princess bridge is closed, walk ahead for ¼ mile. Take the first right onto Irwell Street/Quay Street. Cross the river, and continue winding ahead. After ¼ mile and just past some elegant brick houses on your left, turn right onto Lower Byrom Street. In 200 yards pass *The Manchester Museum of Science and Industry* on your right, before reaching Liverpool Road. Turn left and immediately right.

20. You are now on Duke Street with the traditional but upgraded *Oxnoble, Public House* on the far corner. To the left of here is where the Romans built a fort when they first came to the area. At this point, if you wish learn more about *Roman Castlefield*, see some Roman remains and find out about the Roman fort which gave Castlefield its name, take the second left off Duke Street into Beaufort Street and walk up to a small park on your left, where you will be able to find out more.

21. Otherwise, continue along Duke Street. At the bottom, walk under a railway arch and bear right keeping under a higher railway line. With a small car park on your left bear left and continue under another arch to find yourself back at the centre of *Castlefield* with Merchants Bridge to your right.

    Return from here to your car or to the metro, depending on the way you came. You may however wish to visit one of the many establishments in the vicinity for refreshment, before starting your journey home.

Roman Castlefield

The Romans first came to Manchester in 79AD and in order to guard the York to Chester Roman road they built a timber fort on an outcrop between The River Irwell and River Medlock. The fort, in what is now Castlefield, was called Mamucium – meaning 'A hill shaped like a breast'. It was later rebuilt in stone and at its peak it garrisoned up to 1,000 troops. The Romans left in AD 410. Although nothing is left of the original fort, after much archaeological investigation, a section of the stone fort including the North Gate, was reconstructed in 1984 as part of the United Kingdom's first Urban Heritage Park. You may visit this from Duke Street at the end of your walk if you wish.

Castlefield from the mid 1700s to the present day

In 1765 The Bridgewater Canal was extended from Streford to Castlefield to become the canal's northern terminus. Warehouses were soon built – the first being the Grocers Warehouse which was constructed in the late 1770s and had water powered machinery to enable the lifting of coal from the barges to street level. This building was demolished in the 1960s, although it has been partially rebuilt. Soon after Grocers Warehouse, Merchants Warehouse and Middle Warehouse were also built. Both were next to arms of the canal and it was therefore possible for barges to enter the warehouses directly from the canal so facilitating the unloading of goods into horse drawn carts. A number of basins were also built, including Brindley's original cloverleaf overflow channel. In 1800 The Rochdale Canal joined The Bridgewater Canal at Castlefield although the former's route across the Pennines wasn't completed until 4 years later in 1804.

With the growth of the railways, much of the canal side area declined and became derelict. However, from the 1980s onwards, regeneration has taken place and the area has been transformed. Some of the old warehouses were demolished, but others have been renovated and converted to different uses. Both Merchants Warehouse and Middle Warehouse can still be seen. Merchants Warehouse has been totally refurbished and contains apartments, offices and two local radio stations and even the Grocers Warehouse has been partially rebuilt. Brindley's original cloverleaf overflow channel is now called Potato Wharf, and the whole area has been sympathetically redeveloped with many up-market apartments, restaurants and cafés, built to fit in with the well-landscaped surroundings. The whole area is now vibrant, with new buildings and structures such as the youth hostel on Potato Wharf and Merchants Bridge across The Bridgewater Canal.

Pomona Locks

Pomona Locks

These locks, the only locks on the Bridgewater Canal, replaced the obsolete Hulme Locks in 1995 and make it possible for boats to pass between The Bridgewater Canal and The Manchester Ship Canal via Pomona Dock no. 3. However, apparently it is quite expensive for boaters to use the locks. (See photograph on previous page)

Salford Quays

The Manchester Ship Canal Company was established in 1882 with the aim of bringing ocean going vessels from The Mersey Estuary into the heart of Manchester. The canal was finally opened by Queen Victoria in 1894. At the Manchester end of the canal, nine docks were built and these docks and associated quays formed a major part of The Manchester Docks. Pomona Docks, nos. 1 to 5, were on the eastern side, between The Ship Canal and the Bridgewater Canal, and the larger Salford Docks, nos. 7 to 9, were on the north western side of the canal.

At their height, the docks were the third busiest port in Britain with cargo being transported to and from the rest of the world - Canada being one of their biggest trading partners. But in the 1970s the advent of container shipping resulted in the slow decline of the docks - the container ships were simply too large for the canal. The docks finally closed in 1982 and the area became derelict. However, in 1984 Salford City Council bought 220 acres of the land around the docks, and a year later a development plan began to be formulated that finally resulted in the present day Salford Quays.

Between 1986 and 1990 roads, bridges and walkways were built, the area was landscaped and the whole infrastructure of the docks was modified in order to create a centre for tourism and leisure. This included moorings and watersports facilities. Well designed homes were built, originally low rise and later high rise, and a Metrolink branch was also constructed, firstly the Eccles Line and more recently a spur to Media City.

In April 2000 The Lowry Arts Centre was opened between the old docks 8 and 9 (see below), in July 2002 The Imperial war Museum North was opened (also see below) and more recently on pier 9, 200 acres has been developed by Peel Group for mixed use, but concentrating mainly on media organizations, the most prominent one being the BBC. In 2014 a new Granada Studios was opened on the far side of the canal.

The Imperial War Museum North

0161 836 4000 **www.iwm.org.uk**

The Imperial War Museum North was opened in July 2002, in an area of Trafford Park which was very heavily bombed during the Manchester Blitz.

The building, designed by Daniel Libeskind is said to represent a world shattered by war.

The Lowry Bridge

The single span, 92 metre long Lowry Bridge, was opened on 28 April 2000 and provides pedestrian access between The Salford Quays Development including The Lowry Centre and The Imperial War Museum North. It also connects Salford and Trafford, the canal being the boundary between the two boroughs. The bridge has four tubular 30 metre high steel towers which allow the deck to be raised 23 metres above the water for ships to pass. During the bridge's construction, the deck was floated 500 metres along the canal on a special barge from Holland, so that it could be lifted into position. From the bridge you can see Media City to the left of The Lowry Centre.

The Lowry Centre

0843 208 6000 **www.thelowry.com**

The Lowry Centre, designed by James Stirling, was opened in April 2000. It is a multi purpose arts centre and contains The Lyric Theatre which holds 1730 people; the 440 seat Quays Theatre; studios; gallery space and one of the largest collection of Lowry's work in the country. There is a café, a bar and a restaurant. You might also wish to visit the Salford Tourist Office which is to the left inside the entrance. Here you can obtain free information not only about the centre, but also about the whole of Salford Quays. You may even be lucky as the author was, and find a book on The Cheshire Ring! If you have a little more time, pick up a free 'Salford Quays Heritage Trail' and follow what is apparently a '3 mile self guided walk discovering Salford Quays past and present' before continuing on the walk.

The cranes by Ontario Basin

By the traffic lights at the top of Ontario Basin you will see two large 3 ton blue electric cranes. These were originally located on No.6 dock and operated from 1966 to the early 1980s. They were re-erected on their present site in 1988.

Liverpool Road Station and Manchester Museum of Science and Industry

0800 047 8124 **www.scienceandindustrymuseum.org.uk**

Liverpool Road Station was the first passenger station to be built in England, on the first passenger line from Manchester to Liverpool. It began to be used increasingly for goods traffic and by the late 1830s warehouses to the north of the station were used as a store and interchange between rail and road transport. Note the numerous railway lines and viaducts in the area. It is no longer used as a station, but is part of the larger Manchester Museum of Science and Industry, the main entrance of which is a short distance away on Liverpool Road. If you have time and wish to do so, this fascinating museum is definitely worth a visit. It is hoped that recent talk of closing the museum will come to nothing.

Places you may wish to stop for refreshment

The café/bar at the Lowry Centre

The Oxnoble, on The corner of Liverpool Road and Duke Street *0161 834 3321* **www.oxnoblemanchester.co.uk**

A number of establishments near Merchants Bridge, including **Dukes 92**: *0161 839 8642* **www.dukes92.com**

WALK 2
Old Trafford to Stretford

Stretford – Longford Park – Old Trafford – The Bridgewater Canal – Stretford

Starting point	**Hancock Street, off the A56, Stretford. Grid reference: 796938**
Length	**5½ miles**
Allow	**Approximately 2½ hours**
Map	**OS Explorer 277**
By car	**If coming from Manchester on the A56, pass the junction of Edge Lane/Kingsway in Stretford, then take the second left into Crossford Street. This is after a petrol station. Take the second right into Hancock Street and park at the end where the road bends to the left.** **If coming along the A56 from the south, you cannot turn right into Crossford Street. Instead, at the large roundabout just to the Manchester side of the M60/A56 junction, bear left up the A5181 Barton Road – following the sign to Urmston. At the first main traffic lights turn right down Kingsway, then at the A56 traffic lights, turn right again, onto the left hand lane of the southbound A56 with the Arndale Centre on your right. Take the second left into Crossford Street and follow the instructions above**
By Metrolink	**Leave the tram at Stretford Station. Cross Edge Lane, turn right and go over the canal bridge. Walk down the slope to your left, going back on yourself parallel to the road to reach the canal. At the end of the walk you leave here at direction no. 14.* Turn right and walk along the canal bank for about ⅓ mile. Immediately after passing Watch House Cruising Club come off the canal to your right, walk through a car park, and turn left to go down some steps to continue the walk from the canal bridge in Direction 1**

This walk is varied in character. Off the canal, Longford Park and Gardens are a pleasant surprise and there is the added interest of two major sporting venues - Old Trafford Football Stadium home to Manchester United, and Old Trafford Cricket Club. The canal section passes through Trafford Park, past Waters Meeting where the Leigh Branch of the canal joins the main canal and alongside Stretford Marina.

The Walk

. Bear left at the end of Hancock Street and walk under the canal and railway bridges. Pass Stretford Cemetery on your left. In about 250 yards after the bridge you reach an unsurfaced car park which is also on your left. Turn into this, and cross diagonally to go into a large playing field.

2. Once on the playing field, which can be wet at times, turn slightly to the left and cross over in a northerly direction. You want to walk parallel to, and about 50 yards from the left hand side of the field, making for a footpath sign which is about 350 yards away in front of some houses at the far side. This is to the left of Stretford Grammar School which you should keep to your front right.

3. At the far side of the field take the footpath which bends to the left between the houses. At the end of the path, bear right to walk along Meadow Close until you come to Granby Road. Turn right at Granby Road and in under 100 yards and just before the entrance to Stretford Grammar School take a footpath to your left. This path leads you between houses onto Edge Lane.

4. Turn right at Edge Lane. Walk past the imposing Rylands Hall on your left, cross the road at the pedestrian lights and continue in the same direction. At the corner with Cromwell Road, enter Longford Park to the left of the lodge. Once in the park, walk along the main tree lined path. After passing paths on both the left and right, the main path bears slightly right

Rylands Hall, Edge Lane (now the Church of Christ)

and you come to the large arched entrance to 'The Hall Garden' on your left. If by any chance you end up on the wrong path, look for the arched garden entrance, there is no mistaking it once you are there!

The arch leading to Longford Park Gardens

5. Go through the arch into the Longford Park Gardens. The plan of the old Longford Hall on the side of the arch tells you that the gardens occupy the site of the old hall. Walk through and enjoy these gardens, going forward with the arch behind you until you come to Pets Corner on your left. Keeping the green railings on your left, bear right here then left and continue ahead until you reach a recently built curved brick back wall to the gardens. If you have deviated too much to the right, still make for this wall at the back. It is distinctive brick with yellow surrounds, and to the left of it are some old buildings, possibly the stables. At the far right side of this curved wall is an exit from the formal gardens. Go through here and turn left down a path.

6. Follow this path with a wire fence and hedge to your left and field to your right. Walk ahead towards some buildings, which are at the end of the field in the far left corner of the park. When you reach the buildings you will see a car park, Firswood Community Centre, and The Beacon Centre. Leave the park here at Kings Road Circus.

7. Cross the roundabout diagonally to reach a row of shops on the opposite corner. Go through an opening between the two blocks of shops, and under a brick arch onto Rutland Avenue. In slightly less than 100 yards take the first left along Headingley Drive and then the first right along Wilton Avenue. You soon come to a T-junction at Warwick Road. At the time of writing, opposite you there are a number of run down factories/offices, although with the Metrolink extensions, the whole area may well be redeveloped. Turn left along Warwick Road and you will soon come to a right hand bend with Old Trafford Metrolink Station on your left. Note the Metrolink works and sidings ahead, which are on what was formerly a continuation of Warwick Road.

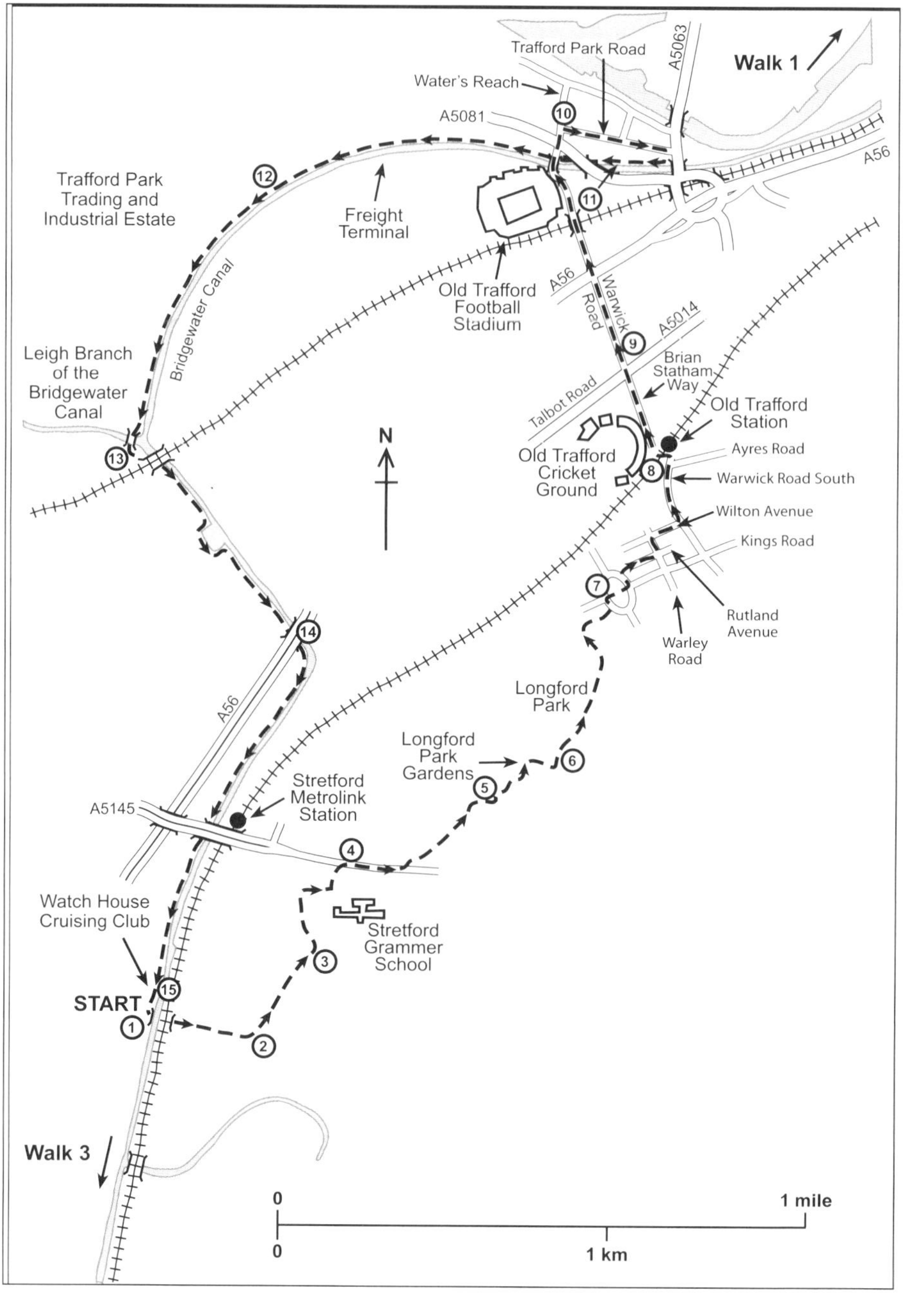
Trafford Park Road
A5063
Walk 1
Water's Reach
A5081
A56
Trafford Park Trading and Industrial Estate
Freight Terminal
Old Trafford Football Stadium
A56
Warwick Road
A5014
Bridgewater Canal
Leigh Branch of the Bridgewater Canal
Brian Statham Way
Talbot Road
Old Trafford Station
N
Old Trafford Cricket Ground
Ayres Road
Warwick Road South
Wilton Avenue
Kings Road
Rutland Avenue
Warley Road
Longford Park
A56
Longford Park Gardens
Stretford Metrolink Station
A5145
Watch House Cruising Club
Stretford Grammer School
START
Walk 3
0
1 mile
0
1 km
1
2
3
4
5
6
7
8
9
10
11
12
13
14
15

8. Turn left and cross the metro line. This should be reasonably straight forward, unless you are there on a match day, in which case you may have to go round a number of metal barriers before crossing the line. You may wish to find out beforehand whether there is a football or cricket match being played. Once over the metro track, continue in a straight line down Brian Statham Way. Pass Old Trafford Cricket Ground which is on your left and has recently undergone extensive rebuilding. You soon cross over Talbot Road after which you can see Trafford Town Hall on your left.

9. Continue in the same direction along what is now Warwick Road again and in just over 350 yards cross the A56 Chester Road. Keep ahead along Sir Matt Busby Way to pass Old Trafford Football Stadium, the home of Manchester United Football Club on your left. The stadium dominates the whole area, and you may wish to look around and soak up the atmosphere. Even on non-match days it is often busy with people who have come to visit. Once you are past the stadium entrance, walk ahead, to cross the canal. The Football Hotel, which was opened in 2015, can be seen beside the water on your right. Immediately after crossing the bridge, walk straight ahead across Warfside Way.

10. Almost immediately after Wharfside Way and just before The Premier Inn, turn right down Trafford Wharf Road which is no longer blocked off from the main road system at this end. Continue along here past a parking area and big old warehouses on your right. After slightly under 200 yards join a one way system and continue in the same direction. Over the road to your left you will soon see an interesting anchor sculpture and the Trafford Park sign. Pass the large 'Liverpool Warehousing Co.' warehouse on your right. Immediately past its far corner you will see some steps going down to the right which you will descend. Once down by the canal turn right to walk with the water to your left for 2½ miles.

11. After about 250 yards walk under a bridge carrying the A5081 almost immediately followed by another bridge this time carrying Sir Matt Busby Way. The Football Hotel is on the right between the two bridges. You then pass Manchester United's Old Trafford Football Stadium which overlooks the canal on your left. On the old wall here, you can see mooring pins to remind you of the time when barges travelled down from collieries around Worsley, Wigan and Leigh to deliver coal to Trafford Park Power Station. This trade continued until 1972.

12. Along this stretch of canal, you walk through Trafford Park once said to be the largest industrial estate in Britain. You pass various transport and container storage facilities, small scale industry and office development interspersed with some slightly desolate areas. To your left for much of this section is a large freight terminal. Although Trafford Park is not as active as in the past, it has adapted over time, and this is possibly the reason for its continued success.

13. Just over 1¼ miles after joining the towpath, keep left to cross the Leigh Branch of the canal at Waters Meeting, Soon the canalside becomes more suburban and as you reach the edge of Stretford, pass a housing development on your right, followed by Stretford Marina.

14. About 350 yards after the marina the towpath passes under the A56 Chester Road bridge. The canal then bends to the right, and about ½ mile after the A56 bridge you reach Edge Lane Bridge. Leave here if you came by metro.

Watch House Cruising Club

15. About ⅓ mile after the bridge you reach the white building belonging to The Watch House Cruising Club. Note the interesting metal sign on the far side of the buildings. Immediately after passing Watch House Cruising Club turn right through the car park then keep right descending in front of some cottages to reach the road. Turn right to return to your car.

Longford Park and Gardens

At 22 acres this is the largest municipal park in Trafford. The hall was built and the grounds were laid out in the 1850s for John Rylands, the cotton merchant and benefactor of amongst other places, the John Rylands Library in Manchester. Stretford Urban District Council bought the land in 1911 and in 1912 it became public park. The original stable buildings and coach house are still standing and the gardens occupy the site of the old hall.

Old Trafford Cricket Ground

Home to Lancashire Cricket Club and host to test matches.

Old Trafford Football Stadium

Home to Manchester United Football Club.

Trafford Park

Before The Manchester Ship Canal opened in 1894, Trafford Hall with its surrounding parkland was the country seat of the De Trafford Family whose roots go back to the 11th century. The construction of the Ship Canal made the hall uninhabitable, so the family sold the estate. It was bought by the developer James Hoole, who along with Marshall Stevens of the Manchester Ship Canal Company, created Trafford Park. This was said to be the world's first industrial estate. At its height, during World War 270,000 people were employed at Trafford Park, with transport for both freight and passengers being provided not only by the canal but also internally by a gas powered tramway. Although it is not as busy as in former years, Trafford Park has adapted over time and there is still considerable activity including industrial and office development in the area.

Waters Meeting

The canal which joins from the right at Waters Meeting is the Leigh Branch of The Bridgewater Canal. This was the original stretch of canal which was built by The Duke of Bridgewater in order to carry coal to Manchester from his coalfields at Worsley. It also leads to the Bridgewater Canal's junction with the Leeds and Liverpool Canal at Leigh. Apparently there is a vortex sculpture hidden among the bushes here, but the author has not managed to locate it!

Bridge over the Leigh Branch of the Bridgewater Canal at Waters Meeting

The Watch House Cruising Club

The Watch House Cruising Club is said to be the oldest building in Stretford. It was originally a farmhouse but after the canal was built became a watch or lookout post. In the days of horse drawn transport on the canal, whenever a fly boat was seen coming, new horses were prepared here so reducing the time it took to stop and change the horses. In the 1950s The Watch House was a base for a horse-drawn hotel boat operation which operated countrywide. This historic white building can be seen from the Metro line.

WALK 3

Stretford to Brooklands

Stretford – The Bridgewater Canal – Brooklands – Sale – Worthington Park – Sale Water Park - Chorlton Ees – Stretford

Starting point	**Hancock Street, off the A56, Stretford. Grid reference: 796938**
Length	**6½ miles**
Allow	**2½-3 hours**
Map	**OS Explorer 277**
By car	**If coming from Manchester on the A56, pass the junction of Edge Lane/Kingsway in Stretford, then take the second left into Crossford Street. This is opposite The Arndale centre and after a petrol station. Take the second right into Hancock Street and park at the end where the road bends to the left.** **If coming along the A56 from the south, you cannot turn right into Crossford Street. Instead, at the large roundabout just to the Manchester side of the M60/A56 junction, bear left up the A5181 Barton Road – following the sign to Urmston. At the first main traffic lights turn right down Kingsway, then at the A56 traffic lights, turn right again, onto the left hand lane of the southbound A56 with the Arndale Centre on your right. Take the second left into Crossford Street and follow the above instructions**
By Metrolink	**If you wish to travel by metrolink it is suggested you take the tram to Sale Station, cross both the metro and canal bridges and walk down to your right to join the canal side by Sale Waterside. You would then start and finish the walk at the end of no. 3***

This is a more varied and 'greener' walk than you might initially expect to find so close to Manchester city centre. The canal section passes through the

Mersey Valley followed by a mixed urban landscape which includes the Waterside development in Sale. The Metrolink line runs parallel to this stretch of canal and you pass three stations, with Stretford Station just to the north. This walk therefore can be reached easily by public transport. The return journey is a walk of two halves Initially you walk along pleasant streets containing older suburban housing and through the hidden gem of Worthington Park. After crossing the M60 on one of two iconic suspension footbridges you come to the second 'half' of the return. Here you walk through Sale Water Park, The Mersey Valley and Chorlton Ees which are all delightful.

The Walk

1. From your car, turn left at the bottom of Hancock Street, and keeping left, leave the road and walk up directly in front of some cottages. Once past them, continue to keep left through a small car park. Walk up some steps to the canal bank and with Watch House Cruising Club on your left, turn right. You will walk for 2 miles with the water on your left before leaving the canal after bridge 34, Brooklands Bridge. The whole of this section of canal has a wide towpath and it is easy, fast walking. However, it can get busy and you should beware of cyclists. Along much of this stretch you will see boats moored on the far side of the canal.

2. Between Hancock Street and Dane Road the canal passes through The Mersey Valley, crossing the River Mersey on the Barfoot Aqueduct. You then pass under the M60. This first stretch of canal to Dane Road bridge is pleasant with open space on either side.

3. After almost ¾ mile walk, under Dane Road bridge and immediately pass the *Bridge Inn* on your right, which has a sitting out area. After a while you come to a pleasant development of apartments and town houses on your right whilst on your left the land is of mixed use. About half a mile after Dane Road bridge the canal side opens out as you reach *Sale Waterside*. If you wish

The Bridgewater Canal at Dane Road Bridge

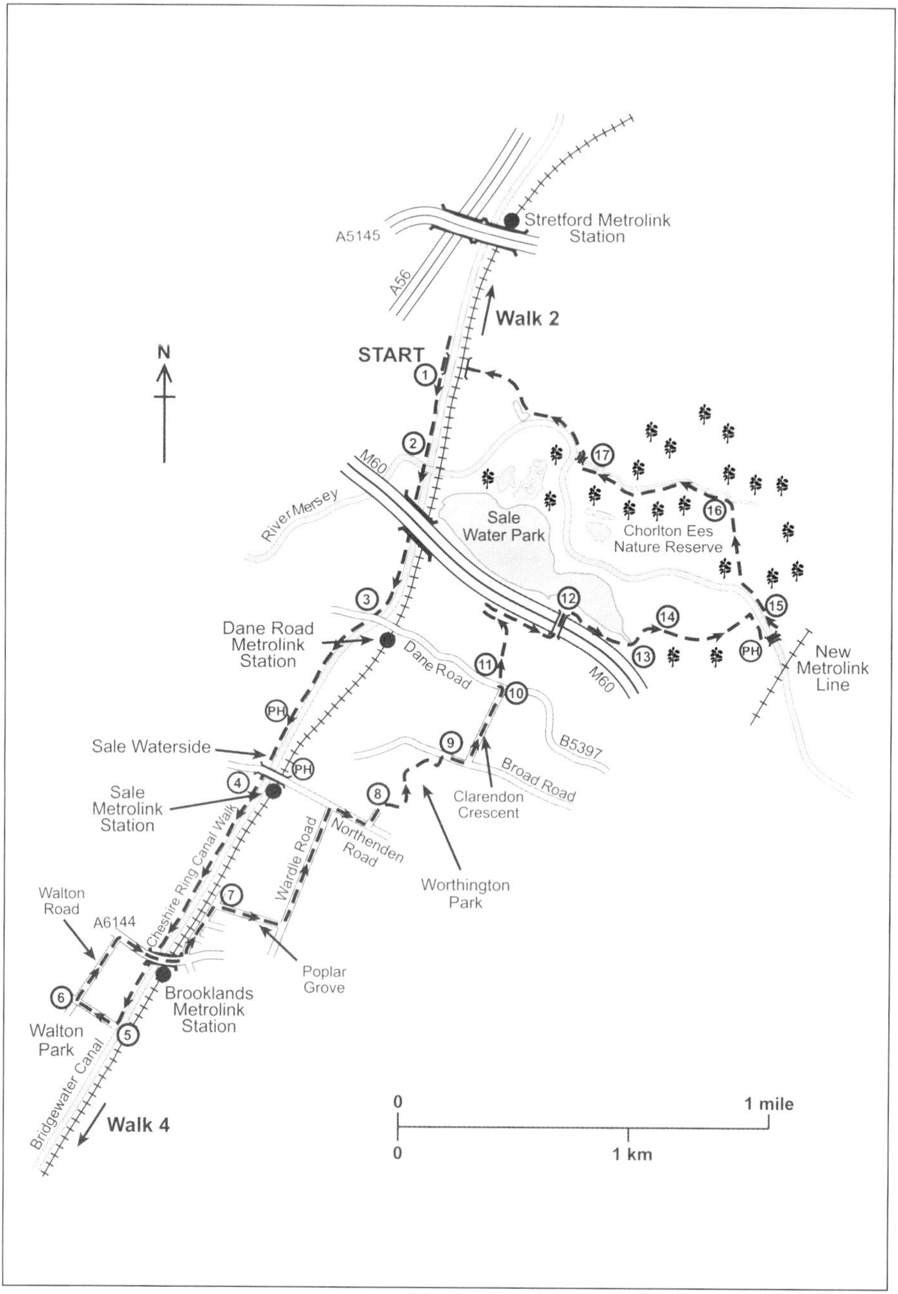
Stretford Metrolink Station
A5145
A56
Walk 2
N
START
M60
River Mersey
Sale Water Park
Chorlton Ees Nature Reserve
Dane Road Metrolink Station
Dane Road
M60
New Metrolink Line
PH
B5397
Broad Road
Sale Waterside
Sale Metrolink Station
Clarendon Crescent
Northenden Road
Wardle Road
Cheshire Ring Canal Walk
Worthington Park
Walton Road
A6144
Poplar Grove
Brooklands Metrolink Station
Walton Park
Bridgewater Canal
Walk 4
0
1 mile
0
1 km

to break your journey, there are a number of restaurants and pubs and *The Railway Inn*, a friendly local, is up a road to the right, if you're wanting a quick drink. Across the canal is *The Kings Ransome Public House* and elsewhere in Sale town centre there are numerous other establishments. Start and finish the walk here if you have come by Metrolink.*

Sale Waterside

Looking south along the canal from Sale

4. Once under the road bridge in Sale you pass an old boat pulley on your right then walk past Springfield Primary School and Sale church, also on your right. In approximately half a mile, after passing well kept terraces followed by a cemetery on your right, you walk under Brooklands Bridge. This stretch between Sale and Brooklands has boats moored along the far bank, possibly associated with Sale Cruising Club which owns premises and land here. Go under Brooklands Bridge and then walk past the other half of the cemetery. At the end of the railings, and about ¼ mile after the bridge, you come to a gap in the hedge on your right and it is here you leave the canal.

5. Go through into a car park bear right and walk to the right of The School of Gymnastics and Trafford Rowing Club buildings. Keep the towpath directly behind you and the buildings to your left and follow the drive away from the canal. With Walton Park on your left, the driveway becomes Raglan Road and you soon reach Walton Road.

6. Turn right along Walton Road. After about 350 yards turn right into Marsland Road and walk over the canal and railway bridge. At the traffic lights cross over diagonally via a number of pedestrian crossings to reach the right hand corner of Hope Road. Walk along Hope Road for just over

300 yards, passing The Brooklands Tap Pub, and take the third right into Poplar Grove.

7. Walk about ¼ mile to the end of Poplar Grove, and with Clifton Road ahead of you, turn left onto Wardle Road. Walk along Wardle Road for ⅓ mile to reach the B5166 Northenden Road. Cross over Northenden Road at the traffic lights then turn right to walk along this main road. After about 200 yards, take the second left into Cheltenham Drive. This will lead you into *Worthington Park.*

8. Once you are in the park, follow the main path round to the right, then to the left until you see the base of an old bandstand. Walk towards it, keeping the children's playground (which was initially to your right), behind you. Bear left to walk round the bandstand and now continue ahead, with a field on your right. The path bends to the right. About 150 yards after the bandstand you pass the exit to Whalley Avenue. Do not leave the park here but continue with the field to your right for about another 100 yards until the path widens. Here you bear left to reach the park exit which takes you to Broad Road.

9. Turn right onto Broad Road and walk along a wide pavement for about 150 yards. Cross the road at some point then at the next cross roads turn left into Clarendon Crescent. Walk along Clarendon Crescent passing playing fields initially on your right and in about ¼ mile you reach Dane Road.

10. Cross Dane Road, and turn left. In less than 50 yards turn right into a large vehicular entrance which leads into Priory Gardens. It is also signposted to the 'Trans Pennine Trail and Bridgewater Way', and there is a sign indicating it is a route for cyclists as well as for walkers. This is immediately before a bus stop and opposite Sale Tennis Club.

11. Walk under a vehicle height restriction bar and, a few yards later, go through a gate. Continue ahead and after just over 200 yards from the entrance you will see a narrow path to your right. If you wish to take a short cut, bear right here, and it leads you to the M60 and a bridge over the motorway. If you do not want to take this shortcut, walk about 100 yards further then turn right at a small wooden post. You almost immediately come to the M60 where you will turn right and walk with the motorway on your left for approximately 250 yards to reach a *footbridge over the M60.* Turn left to cross over this bridge.

12. Come down the steps or ramp the other side into *Sale Water Park*. To your left is a water sports centre and *The Boathouse Restaurant*. There are also some public conveniences. At the bottom of the steps turn right, so the building is behind to your left and the bridge and motorway to your right. Cross diagonally ahead left through the car park going down to the side of the lake where you will turn right to take the path with the lake on your left.

Footbridge over the M60

13. At the end of the lake, walk under a pylon, and turn left to go over some stepping stones. They are quite widely spaced so take care especially if you have small children or small dogs. Walk ahead, crossing a major path. Continue in approximately the same direction, bearing right and keeping a minor tributary of the Mersey on your left. If you stray onto the wrong path and need to ask your way, you are making for *Jackson's Boat Inn*.

Jackson's Boat Inn

14. Keeping on this path, bear slightly right and continue with the stream on your left until you rise up slightly onto a more major path and eventually reach the bank of The River Mersey. Here you turn right and in a few yards you will reach Jacksons Bridge on your left and *Jacksons Boat Inn* on your right. Cross Jacksons Bridge, noting the newly constructed bridge carrying the metro line, to your right.

15. Once over the river, turn left to follow the Trans Pennine Trail along the bank of The Mersey. In just over 250 yards the path splits. You may either continue along the river bank, for about ¾ mile until you reach a small bridge, or bear right here to follow the trail through *Chorlton Ees Nature*

Reserve. If you take the recommended latter route, after bearing right, keep to the main path for about 400 yards until you reach a gate. Walk beside the gate and turn left.

16. Walk through a car park and beside another gate onto a wide path which takes you into an attractive mixed, mainly deciduous woodland. Ignore a path that comes from your left and walk along here, following a small tributary on your right for almost ½ mile, until you eventually reach the river bank again. Turn right.

17. Which ever way you have come, you will now cross a small bridge and bear round to the left. The path immediately splits. Do not take the far left hand path that follows the river, but the one just to the right of it which also initially runs parallel to the river. This is still The Trans Pennine Trail. Where you join a slightly wider path, keep ahead left, and shortly after this, your path bears away from the river. Soon after this, pass a small car park followed by a cemetery on the right. Continue under the railway and canal bridges to return to your car. If travelling by metro from Sale Station, go up on your right to the canal bank, turn right and walk along the towpath back to Sale.

Sale Waterside

This canal side development in Sale includes Sale Library and a number of drinking and eating establishments. There is also an attractive waterside area.

Worthington Park

The land was donated by a Mrs. Worthington in 1900. It was originally known as Sale Park but was re-named in 1950 to celebrate the park's Golden Jubilee. It has been redeveloped in a late Victorian planting style, using 27,000 native trees.

Footbridge over the M60

This bridge, a bold architectural statement, is one of two which were constructed when the motorway was widened.

Sale Water Park

Activities such as dinghy sailing, windsurfing, kayaking, and power boating take place on this 42 acre lake.

Chorlton Ees

It is difficult to imagine, but Chorlton Ees was once the site of the old Withington Sewage Works and the walkways were once old sewage channels. The works closed in 1974 and the derelict land was reclaimed and restored under the government scheme 'Operation Eyesore'. Birds that can be found here include goldfinch, linnet, greenfinch, siskin and heron. Reed bunting, whitethroat, blackcap, chiffchaff and goldcrest are now known to breed at Chorlton Ees.

Places to you may wish to stop for refreshment

The Bridge Inn, Dane Road : *0161 962 3030*
The Railway Inn, Sale: *0161 973 8177 A friendly Robinsons local pub.*
The Kings Ransome, Sale: *0161 969 6006*
The Boathouse Restaurant, Sale: *0161 962 0118*
www.theboathousesale.co.uk *A restaurant with a wonderful view over Sale Water Park.*
Jacksons Boat Inn. Jacksons Bridge: *0161 905 2647*
www.jacksonsboatsale.co.uk
The original inn was built in 1666 and in the 1730s was a meeting place for local Jacobites. It was named after a ferry which was run by a Mr. Jackson. The present inn dates from 1800 and the ferry was replaced by a bridge in the 1830s. The pub is said by some to be haunted.

WALK 4
Brooklands to Seamons Moss

Brooklands – The Bridgewater Canal – Broadheath – Seamons Moss – Stamford Brook – Timperley – Brooklands

Starting point	**Trafford Rowing Club car park, Walton Park, Brooklands. Grid reference: 782909**
Length	**Approximately 6 miles**
Allow	**2-2¼ hours**
Map	**OS Explorer 277**
By car	**From the A56, just under ½ mile south of Sale, turn east down the A6144 Marsland Road towards Brooklands. Immediately before a central road crossing and before you reach the canal bridge, turn right along Walton Road. After almost ¼ mile take the first left into Raglan Road. Keep right to enter Walton Park and park in the car park at the end by Trafford Rowing Club. If this is full, park on Raglan Road or even on Walton Road and walk through to the canal which is at the back of the car park. If coming from the south you may alternatively wish to start the walk at the southern end just north of Altrincham. If so, follow the parking instructions on Walk 5 and start the walk mid way through no. 5***

Much of this walk is suburban, but it is 'greener' and more interesting than might originally be thought. The canal section is varied with plenty to look at and although there are some stretches of road, it is a walk with many contrasts, and some pleasant surprises. These include the reed beds around the Stamford Brook development, the footpath along Sinderland Brook, the parkland near Baguley Brook and the well maintained Walton Park. It is relatively quick, easy walking and probably needs stout shoes rather than walking boots.

The Walk

1. From the car park, go through the gap in the hedge to the canal bank and turn right. You will walk with the water to your left for almost 2½ miles before leaving the towpath at bridge 29, Seamons Moss Bridge. The wide path passes behind the gardens of well-hidden houses on the right, and the metro line is to the left of the canal.

2. After Timperley Station and Park Road Bridge you pass a number of moored boats followed by a small industrial estate and some pleasant apartments to your left, and a recreation area to your right. This is Timperley Flood Storage Basin and although there are playing fields here, you are requested not to enter this site! Past here there is a former industrial area to your right - note the old railway arches which you can see through a gap just before a brick wall. After passing the car park to Halfords you reach the imposing A56 Manchester Road Bridge at *Broadheath*, once an important staging point for *packet boats and fly boats*. This bridge was originally built in 1765, rebuilt in 1830 and again in 1907 when the 'hump' was removed in order to allow trams to travel along the A56. The present bridge dates from 1935. To leave the canal here, go up the steps before the bridge leading to Halfords car park.

3. Once under the bridge, pass the back of Atlantic Street Business Park which continues on your right all the way until you leave the canal. The buildings on the left are far more interesting. Walk past a modern office block on the site of a major coal yard which belonged to the Bridgewater Estates followed by an old building which obviously used the canal for transport in the past. You then come to The Budenberg Haus Apartments on the site of the old Budenberg Works. This is a well-designed and much feted, though slightly unusual development.

4. A little further on to your left and a little way back from the canal, you can see the clock tower of the old *Linotype Works*, although this is partially hidden by a recent housing development. Soon after this you pass part of

Old canal side warehouse

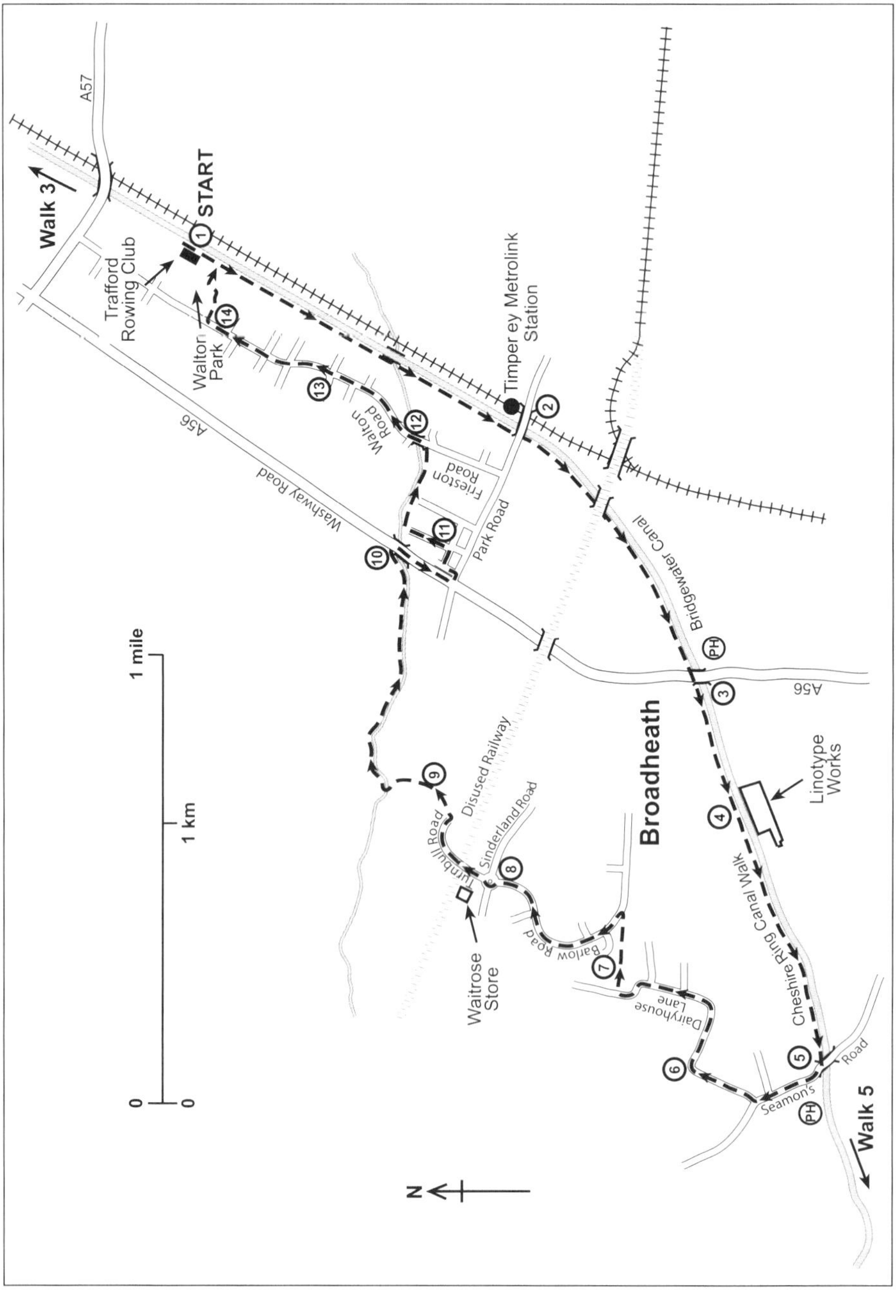

Walk 3
START
Trafford Rowing Club
Walton Park
Timperley Metrolink Station
A57
A56
Washway Road
Walton Road
Frieston Road
Park Road
Bridgewater Canal
PH
Broadheath
Disused Railway
Sinderland Road
Turnbull Road
Linotype Works
Cheshire Ring Canal Walk
Waitrose Store
Barlow Road
Dairyhouse Lane
Seamon's Road
PH
Walk 5
1 mile
1 km
0
0
N
1
2
3
4
5
6
7
8
9
10
11
12
13
14

the original canal frontage of the *Linotype Works*, which they appear to be incorporating into the new development. Walk under a corrugated bridge and past a large pulley on your left, followed by some pleasant modern housing, also on your left. Towards the end of the housing, pass a small marina. The canal bends slightly to the right and a gas pipeline and Seamons Moss Bridge come to view. Just before the bridge leave the canal to your right.

Budenberg Haus Apartments

5. Once on the road, look back to see the narrow old bridge in its original form. Despite a traffic light system, some of the walls by the bridge have been damaged by vehicles. Turn right, to walk along Seamons Road, passing The former Bay Malton Pub on your left. Cross over Atlantic Street. Opposite is the car park to The Trans Pennine Trail, where you may park if you wish to start the walk from here, and also where you will park for Walk 5.* Just over 300 yards after leaving the canal turn right down Dairyhouse Lane, following the Trans Pennine Trail sign. Take care as there is no pavement along this next section.

6. The road bends to the right, and just over 250 yards after the bend you come to cross roads. Here you turn left onto what is still Dairyhouse Lane. Once you have turned left, cross the road to walk on a pavement. After passing The Altrincham Business Park on your right, the road bears left round a small width-restricted chicane. Take great care when walking past the narrow section. Where the road bends back to the right cut across the grass at the corner. At the end of a building on your right turn right down a footpath. Do not go on the path to the left leading to the houses but take the enclosed one to the right leading between houses on your left and the railings at the back of the Business Park on your right.

7. Walk down the footpath for just under 350 yards and at the end of the footpath turn left to walk along Barlow Road for about half a mile. The road gradually bears to the right and although it is a suburban road, the footpath is wide, and it is easy walking. About half way along there is a

small convenience store converted from one of the houses, if you feel you need some sustenance.

8. When you reach a mini roundabout, cross over Sinderland Road at a crossing place just to your left. Walk ahead over a new wide bridge noting a large Waitrose store below to the left. Once over the bridge, the road bears right and you cross Rosefinch Road on your left. Almost immediately after this, (and about 350 yards after the roundabout) turn left down a footpath which takes you along a 'green corridor'. There is a semi-rural feel to this stretch of the walk, with reed beds to your left, and you may wish to sit and enjoy the surroundings.

9. Walk along this attractive footpath for just over 200 yards before crossing over Riverbrook Road to continue ahead along the main path which bears left. Ignore paths to your left and right, and in just over 100 yards after crossing the road, bear right to cross a metal bridge over Sinderland Brook. Once over, turn right to follow the brook on your right, for about ½ mile before reaching the A56. It is pleasant walking along a well made path. Initially Woodhouse Park is on the left but later you will pass the backs of houses on your left and grassy parkland over the brook on your right.

10. When you reach the A56 turn right and walk for about 250 yards to reach the traffic lights. Here you turn left to cross over the busy A56 then continue in the direction you are now facing, along Park Road. Walk by the side of the shops for a few yards then turn left to walk behind the shops. After about 50 yards and opposite a gap between the back of the shops, turn right to walk along Cholmondeley Avenue. You soon reach to Malpas Drive - note the well kept little roundabout in the middle of the road!

11. Turn left along Malpas Drive and in slightly under 200 yards the road bears to the right with an area of parkland on the left. Behind this is the brook you previously followed but it is now known as Baguley Brook. Walk across the grass to reach the side of the brook either from the corner or after walking a little way along the road. At the brook turn right and stay on the path keeping as close to the water on your left as possible, until you reach Frieston Road. To your right is the Park Road Primary School.

12. Turn left onto Frieston Road and cross the brook on a narrow footbridge. This now becomes Walton Road. You have a choice here. If you do not wish to walk ½ mile along Walton Road, turn right once you have crossed

the brook, and when you reach the canal, turn left back along the towpath to return to the car park. However, if you do not wish to retrace your steps, and want to see Walton Park, follow Walton Road ahead.

13. After a few minor bends, Eastway joins in about ¼ mile. Continue in the same direction along Walton Road, and after crossing Marford Crescent (both ends) you reach the gates to Walton Park on your right. This is about ½ mile after crossing Baguley Brook. Turn right into the park.

14. Walton Park is well used and well maintained. Walk ahead, keeping slightly to your left, aiming for the far left corner of the park. Turn left before you reach the tennis courts, then once past the courts turn right – keeping the courts on your right. At the far side of the courts, note the Walton Park Station sign on your left. When you reach the back of the park, with the canal ahead of you behind the hedge, turn left. Walk past the miniature railway and the Trafford Rowing Club on your left to return to the car park and your car.

Broadheath

This was the second stopping place on the journey from Manchester to Runcorn. The 8am boat from Manchester stopped here at 10am to reach Runcorn at 5pm. In the other direction, the boat arrived here at 4pm to reach Manchester at 6pm. Today there are two pubs to your left on the main road, and Broadheath Retail Park over the road to your right. There are also a number of other shops and facilities along the road.

Packet boats and fly boats

The original horse drawn packet boats carried both passengers and up to 112lb of freight. The faster flyboats were introduced to compete with the railways. These travelled non stop day and night and were crewed by 3 men, two working and one sleeping, with horses being changed regularly. When steam boats were introduced in the late 19th century they were manned by 4 crew.

The Linotype Works

This factory, built in 1897, manufactured metal printing type. There were once extensive canal side wharfs and related facilities here as The Bridgewater Canal was used for both receiving the raw materials and distributing the finished goods. There are well designed 'cottages' on nearby roads which provided housing for Linotype workers. The more senior your job, the larger house you were given.

Places you may wish to stop for refreshment

The Old Packet House, Broadheath *0161 929 1331. This pub provided shelter for packet boat passengers and facilities for goods to be stored.*

Former full canal frontage of the Linotype Works

WALK 5

Seamons Moss to Little Bollington

Seamons Moss – The Bridgewater Canal – Little Bollington – Dunham Massey – Dunham Town – The Trans Pennine Trail – Seamons Moss

Starting point	**In the Trans Pennine Trail car park on Seamons Road, Altrincham. Grid reference: 752888**
Length	**4½-5 miles**
Allow	**Approximately 1½ hours (without stops)**
Maps	**OS Explorer 277 and OS Explorer 276**
By car	**From the A56 in Altrincham, turn west along Oldfield Road, about ¼ mile north of the Cresta Court Hotel and the A56/A560 junction. Continue down Oldfield Road, which then becomes Seamons Road, for about a mile. Go over the narrow canal bridge, as directed by the traffic lights, bear sharp left then right and park on your left in The Trans Pennine Trail car park. If you wish to park in Little Bollington (though parking is limited) follow parking instructions for Walk 6 and start this walk in the middle of Direction 6***

This walk could be said to have almost everything. It is a food and drink lover's paradise, and if you throw in the most visited National Trust Property in the North West, lovely views, and old cottages with well tended gardens, you could spend the best part of a day being diverted from what you had originally planned to do! There is even a micro brewery you may wish to visit. The downside is that parts of it can get very busy at times, so perhaps it is best to avoid sunny summer weekend afternoons and bank holidays. However, as you will start away from the busiest section, parking should hopefully be less of a problem. If you wish to start at the southern end, which admittedly is easier to reach, it should still be possible to park somewhere in Little Bollington.

It is suggested that if you wish to visit Dunham Massey House, Gardens and Deer Park, you give yourself at least an extra hour or two.

The Walk

1. Leave the Trans Pennine Trail car park and turn right onto Seamons Road. Walk back towards the canal, taking care as it can be busy. Where the road bends to the left, walk down to your right onto the towpath.

2. Once on the towpath, turn right and you will walk along the canal, with the water on your left for approximately 2 miles, finally leaving at bridge 26A, Bollington Underbridge. This is a pleasant stretch of canal, especially if you are doing the walks going out from the centre of Manchester, as suggested in the book, because at last you leave the town and are in the countryside. Apart from some short urban and industrial stretches around Northwich and Middlewich, the towpath is through the countryside all the way to Hall Green near Kidsgrove.

First glimpse of the countryside

3. After walking along the towpath for about ⅓ mile the canal bends to the right and then to the left. In slightly less than a mile after joining the canal, you pass under the bridge at Dunham Town, which is where you will cross over the canal on your return journey. Continue behind some exclusive houses on your right, walk under another bridge and about ½ mile past the houses, walk over the *Dunham Underbridge* which carries the road to Dunham Woodhouses. Take care whilst crossing this as the footway is narrow.

4. Approximately ¼ mile further on, the canal goes over *The River Bollin Aqueduct*, the site of a huge breach in 1971. It is a surprisingly wide aqueduct with another bridge over the river beneath it. This is the boundary between Trafford in Greater Manchester and Warrington. The canal now widens slightly. Much of this section is slightly above the surrounding countryside and gives you good views all around. Note *Bollin Mill* to your left which you will pass later in the walk.

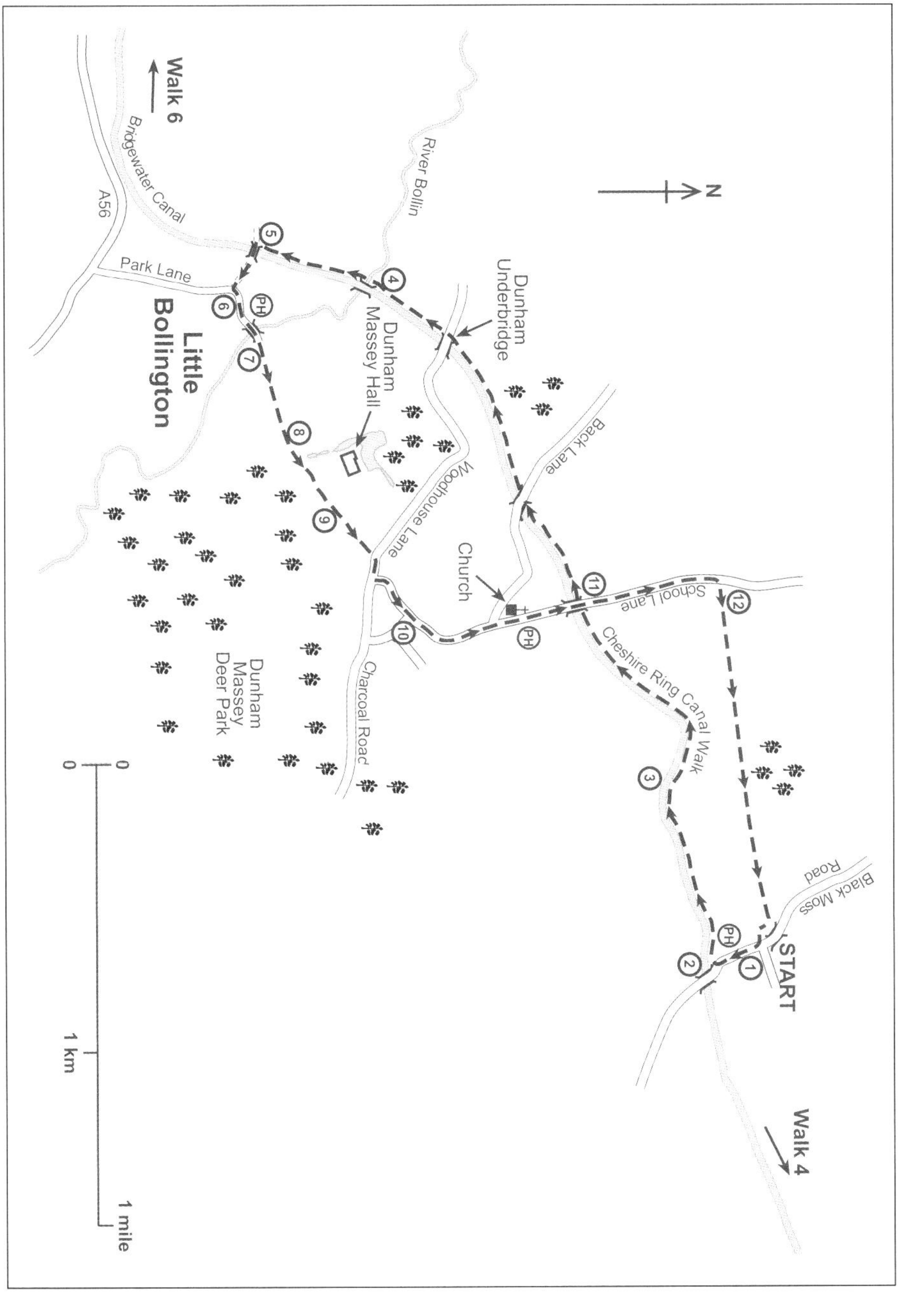
Walk 6
Bridgewater Canal
A56
River Bollin
N
Park Lane
Little Bollington
PH
Dunham Underbridge
Dunham Massey Hall
Back Lane
Woodhouse Lane
Church
School Lane
PH
Cheshire Ring Canal Walk
Charcoal Road
Dunham Massey Deer Park
Black Moss Road
PH
START
Walk 4
1
2
3
4
5
6
7
8
9
10
11
12
0
0
1 km
1 mile

5. About ¼ mile after crossing the River Bollin you leave the canal down some concrete steps to your right. Be careful not to miss this as it is not very clear. The steps are just before the canal narrows slightly on the left to go over Bollington Underbridge, and also quite close to an electricity pylon on the right. If you come to where the electricity cables cross the canal it means you have gone too far! At the bottom of the steps turn left under the bridge and in a little under 200 yards you reach the small green in the centre of Little Bollington.

6. Little Bollington is an attractive estate village. Turn left at the green, with a large half timbered building set back from the road on your left. Start here if coming from the south* Walk past the 'dog-friendly' *Swan With Two Nicks* on your left. About 100 yards further on, cross the River Bollin on a narrow, footbridge. Note *Bollin Mill* on your left.

The Swan with Two Nicks – Little Bollington

7. Once over the bridge, ignore both the footpath sign to your right along the river and the driveway (signposted as a restricted byway) which bears round to the left but continue straight ahead to go onto an enclosed tree lined track which leads to *Dunham Massey*. Walk along this straight path towards the house and parkland for just over 400 yards, enjoying the views all around.

8. At the end of the path, climb over a step stile, and you are now in *Dunham Massey Deer Park*. If you are fortunate you will see numerous deer, and not too many people. Pass the old mill on your left, and the main house will soon come into view. To your left there is a café and restaurant in the stable block although it can get busy at peak times. However there is now another café and shop in a new visitors centre slightly further away by the car park. Also on your left are *Dunham Massey House and Gardens* which you may wish to visit. The house is only open in the summer, but the gardens are now open all year, and the Winter gardens are a delightful recent attraction. You must obtain a ticket from the visitor centre before going into either the hall or gardens.

Dunham Massey Hall

9. To continue the walk, pass a wide path leading to the main door of the house on your left and walk directly ahead keeping just to the right of a stone plinth with a lion on top. Do not bear right down the wider path. Walk ahead along this tree lined path (Smithy Drive) for about 350 yards before reaching a white gate and step stile leading on to Woodhouse Lane. Once over the stile, turn right and in about 50 yards, cross the road with care and turn left into what is still Woodhouse Lane.

10. Just after the big tree and where Charcoal Road joins from the right, pass *Dog Farm* on your left. There is a café here called Dunham Barn which has pleasant outside seating. If you want to visit *Dunham Micro Brewery* turn right by the tree and follow the signs. However, to continue the walk, carry on ahead to reach the centre of the small estate village of *Dunham Town*, which is made up of small cottages, with well tended summer gardens, a tiny church and an even tinier shop. Pass Back Lane on your left, keeping the small church to your left. *The Axe and Cleaver* ahead on the right serves food for most of the day.

11. About ½ mile after leaving the Dunham Park cross over the canal, and about ⅓ mile further on you come to a bridge over the track of an old railway. Just before the bridge, go down some steps to your left.

12. At the bottom of the steps, turn right onto the wide track, once the line of a railway and now part of *The Trans Pennine Trail*. Go under the bridge and you will walk along here for ¾ mile to return to the car park and your car.

Dunham Underbridge

There have been a number of leaks here over the years including a recent one which necessitated the road closure whilst some new supports and a run off channel were built.

The River Bollin Aqueduct

In 1971 there was a breach in the embankment over the valley approaching the aqueduct, resulting in the original stone aqueduct being swept away. As a consequence, this section of the canal was closed for two years. The repairs and construction of the present aqueduct apparently cost about £250,000. The Bridgewater Canal Society was formed as a result of this breach.

Bollin Mill

This was once a flour mill, its large wheel using water from the River Bollin to grind the corn. It was later a fertilizer store and has now been converted into upmarket apartments.

Dunham Massey Hall, Gardens and Deer Park

This was once the seat of The Earl of Stamford The blood line died out in the mid-20th century and it was taken over by The National Trust in 1976. The house was originally built in 1616 by George Booth but was remodelled in the 18th century by John Norris. The deer park, which has been parkland since the middle ages, was landscaped by the second Earl of Warrington, George Booth. Many of the oak trees date from the 17th century and apparently it has the greatest concentration of old oak trees in the North West. The 193 acres of parkland continues to be well stocked with fallow deer, many of which are brave enough to venture close to the house. The gardens to the side of the house are a pleasure to walk round, and they are open all year. The Winter Gardens, the largest in the north west, are a relatively recent addition and are well worth a visit. Note the 18th century orangery and the delightful new rose garden.
www.nationaltrust.org.uk/dunham-massey

Dunham Town

Dunham Town, like Little Bollington and also Dunham Woodhouses nearby, is a Dunham estate village. Note the red painted woodwork on the houses and farms in the area which indicates they are estate buildings.

Dunham Micro Brewery

The brewery produces up to twelve 'craft' beers which are sold to local outlets. Open most days to visitors but check times. To reach it, turn right by the big tree in Dunham Town. (Tel: 0161 929 0663)

The Trans Pennine Trail

This section of the Trans Pennine Trail follows the line of The Warrington and Altrincham Junction Railway, which opened from Timperley Junction to Warrington in 1853. It was almost immediately re-named the Warrington and Stockport Railway and connected Manchester with Liverpool via a southerly route. After being taken over by the London and North West Railway, it closed to passengers in the 1960s and now forms the Broadheath to Latchford section of The Trans Pennine Trail.

Places you may wish to stop for refreshment

Dunham Massey Restaurant and Tea rooms
www.nationaltrust.org.uk/dunham-massey
Turn left just before the path to the house. This is situated in a large room above the stable block and thought by the author to be one of the better National Trust restaurants and tea rooms. However, it can get busy. There is also now another café in the Visitors Centre near the car park.

The Swan with Two Nicks, Little Bollington: 0161 928 2914
www.swanwithtwonicks.co.uk
This attractive old pub, which welcomes dogs, was apparently named after the custom of putting two nicks in the beak of a swan, to establish its ownership. It is said that Dick Turpin frequently stopped here on his journeys to the north.

Dog Farm, Dunham Town
At the present time there is a small craft shop and tearooms here. It is pleasant to sit outside in the summer.

The Axe and Cleaver, Dunham Town: *0161 928 3391*
This is a large pub which serves food for most of the day. It has a relaxed atmosphere and attentive service.

WALK 6

Little Bollington to Lymm

Little Bollington – The Bridgewater Canal – Lymm – Agden – Little Bollington

Starting point	**Little Bollington. Grid reference: 729870**
Length	**7 miles**
Allow	**2½-3 hours**
Map	**OS Explorer 276**
By car	**Where the M56 Junction 7/8 joins the A56 and A556 at the Bowdon roundabout, take the A56 towards Lymm. After about a mile, turn right to Little Bollington. There is limited parking here, but if you are returning to 'The Swan with Two Nicks' afterwards, there is parking behind the pub. You may however choose to begin the walk in Lymm, In this case, park in Pepper Street Car Park and start and finish at Direction 8***

This is a very pleasant, undemanding walk with some quiet rural stretches and good views. It also has the benefit of offering sustenance of all types half way through the walk in the attractive small town of Lymm.

It should be noted that the route of the proposed new HS2 rail line cuts across the canal and lanes near Agden Bridge. As there may then be temporary closure of parts of the route, it is suggested you carry a map.

The Walk

1. Facing the small green in Little Bollington with the A56 behind you, and '*The Swan with Two Nicks*' ahead, turn left down a cobbled lane. At the right hand corner of the lane is a large half timbered house which is set back from the road. Walk down the lane for just over 150 yards, go under

the canal bridge and take the steps on your right which lead up to the canal.

2. At the towpath turn right and you will walk for just over 3 miles with the water on your left to leave the canal in Lymm after passing under bridge 23. Soon after starting the walk you can hear and then see the A56 to your left. As the main road comes closer you can see the *Old Number 3 Pub* on the opposite bank but unfortunately you can't reach it! Pass under Agden Bridge noting an old crane on your left and you come to the start of extensive moorings for Lymm Cruising Club. The boats, lined up along the canal, are attractive and varied. It is here that the new HS2 rail line may cross the canal in the future. You then walk past a large boatbuilding yard and marina followed by 'Hesford Marine Stores and Chandlery'.

3. After the boatyards, you pass *The Barn Owl Pub* on the opposite side of the canal. Even though it is said that a bell can be rung to call a ferryman to come and take you across the canal here, the author was unable to locate it. Pass some prefabricated buildings soon followed on your left by a building made up of a house and warehouse which was once a *hospital for canal horses.*

4. Almost immediately after the former canal horse hospital, walk over Agden Underbridge, although unless you look down carefully, you may not be aware of this. You will now see Spud Wood on your left and walk under a pedestrian bridge. Once past this bridge which leads to Spud Wood, you come to some houses on your right with gardens backing onto the canal. After passing Oughtrightington Community Orchard on your right you walk under *Lloyd Bridge.* Outrightington Church, the spire of which can be seen from a number of miles away, is now to your left.

5. Between here and Lymm, the canal becomes more interesting, curving round to the left, with overhanging trees in places. Less than a mile further on, and after some reed beds to your left, you reach the outskirts of Lymm.

The canal side coming into Lymm - looking east

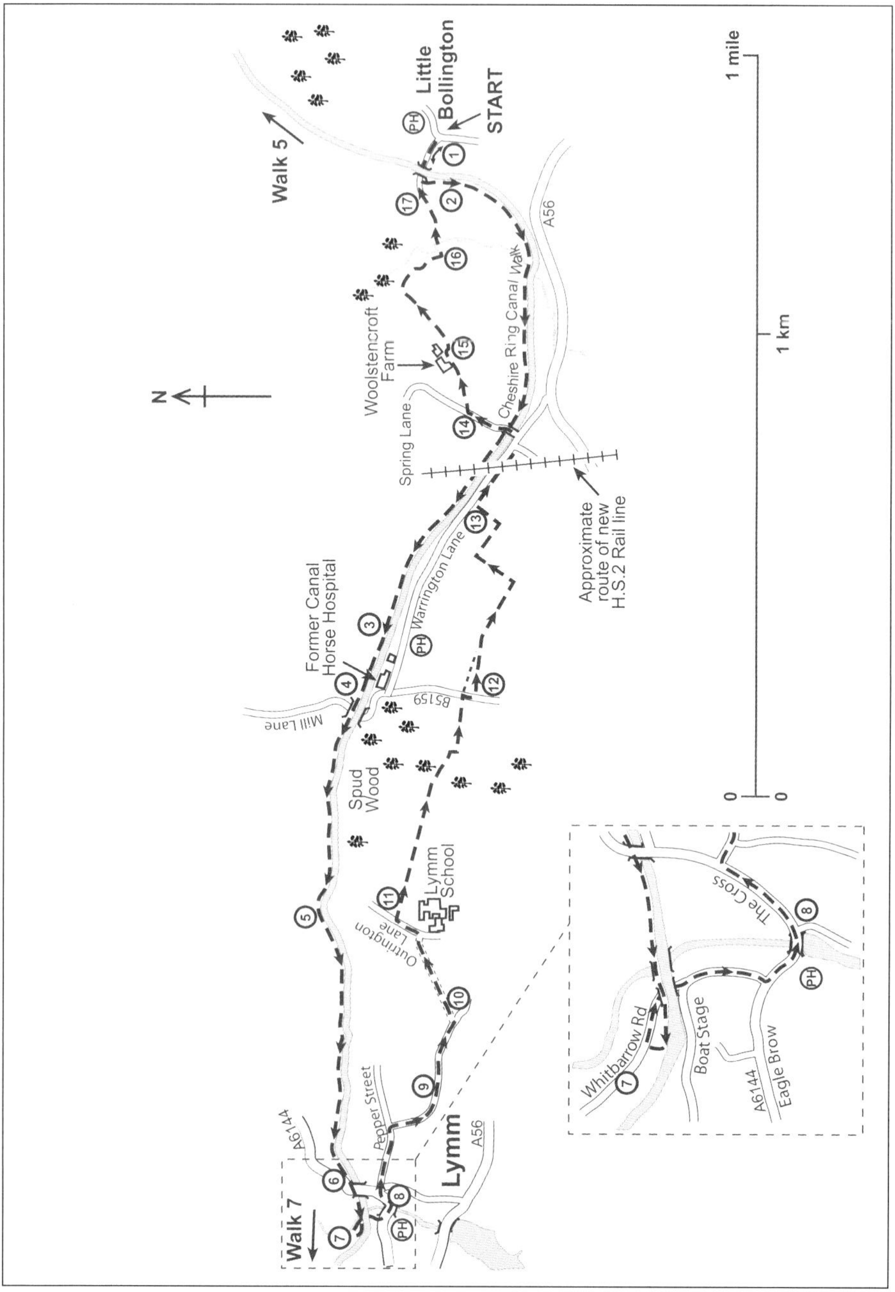
Walk 5
Little Bollington
START
PH
N
Woolstencroft Farm
Cheshire Ring Canal Walk
A56
Spring Lane
Approximate route of new H.S.2 Rail line
Warrington Lane
Former Canal Horse Hospital
PH
B5159
Mill Lane
Spud Wood
Lymm School
Outrington Lane
Pepper Street
A6144
Lymm
A56
Walk 7
PH
Whitbarrow Rd
Boat Stage
A6144
Eagle Brow
The Cross
PH
0
1 mile
1 km

Before the main bridge over the road, you walk past some pleasant modern dwellings on both sides of the canal, the ones just before the bridge on the right are of a particularly varied character. You will also pass Lymm Cruising Club on your left. Next to their slipway is a small arm of the canal which once led to an unloading tunnel. This is now known as Lymm Tunnel.

6. Go under bridge 23 in Lymm, after which you pass a white house on your right, where apparently the son of a famous puppeteer lived for a number of years. Walk over Whitbarrow Underbridge (which you may not be aware of!) then come off the Canal to your right, opposite a car park and just before The Bridgewater Club . This small stretch of canal is especially attractive. There are many boats moored here and a popular market is held every Thursday in the car park opposite.

Looking back towards the bridge at Lymm

7. When you reach the road, turn right. To your immediate left is a steep gorge which has been made into a linear park leading to Lymm Dam. Staying on the road, go under the canal bridge and past a number of small shops to reach the centre of *Lymm*. Turn left opposite The Spread Eagle Public House and follow the road round to your left, walking over the wide cobbled bridge which crosses the gorge. Continue round to the left and cross the road at the zebra crossing.

Lymm

8. Walk towards the *17th century Lymm Cross*. Walk up past the cross then ahead into cobbled Pepper Street which is the road immediately opposite, not the one which bends back up to the right. Pass a car park on your left* and after walking along this road for just over 300 yards, turn right at the

end of an old stone wall topped by a fence and hedge. You are now on The Peppers. The road bends to the right, but instead of following it, continue walking ahead, past bollards onto what now becomes the narrower Longbutt Lane. This lane bears left and just after passing Orchard Avenue on your left you will walk beside an old 'farm type' gate and continue ahead in the same direction.

9. Cross Scholars Green Lane, on which there is well laid out modern housing, and continue ahead on the footpath, which, although passing between houses, has a distinctly rural feel. At the end of this lane, walk through two more gates to cross another part of Scholars Green Lane, and keep ahead once more. You are still on Longbutt Lane.

10. After just under 150 yards and almost opposite Grammar School Road on the right, you will see a footpath sign on your left which you follow. This takes you along a well surfaced and defined path through a field for just under ¼ mile. You are making for Lymm School and Outrightington Church, the spire of which you cannot miss. Once you reach the road turn left. Walk along the pavement for slightly over 100 yards, then when you have passed the church, cross the road and follow the footpath sign over a stile on your right. Do not go down the track beside this, which leads to Lymm O.P. Cricket Club.

The footpath to Outrightington Church

11. Walk along the right hand side of a large field, noting the wide ranging views to your left. At the end of this field, bear right through a small wood. The path dips down and up again past a large pool, to come out into another field. Keeping to the footpath, bear right and then left and walk along the right hand side of the field, resuming your original direction, to reach Burford Lane.

12. Cross Burford Lane, turn right, walk for about 50 yards and just before some houses turn left over a stile to join another footpath. Note that on the OS map this footpath is shown as being opposite the first path. Presumably it was moved to the side of the field by the farmer. Walk

across three fields, keeping to the right of each one and at the far corner of the third field turn left. Walk along this field edge, with the hedge to your right, for about 200 yards (⅔ of the way) then go through a gate on your right. Now walk towards another gate which is just visible half way along the left hand field edge. The 'official' right of way to it is straight ahead then left when in line with the gate.

13. Go through the gate to reach Warrington Lane. Turn right and walk along here for about 350 yards. This road can be busy, and although straight, it is narrow, so take great care. It is proposed that the new HS2 rail line will cross Warrington Lane between your joining it and Agden Bridge, so there may be diversions here in the future. Immediately after a white house and Agden Lane on your right, and by the entrance to Lymm Cruising Club on your left, turn left to cross over Agden Bridge onto Spring Lane.

14. Walk along Spring Lane and in just under 250 yards there is a small sign for Woolstencroft Farm on your right. There should be a footpath sign here, pointing down the drive. Even if there is not a sign, turn right to walk down the road to the farm as it is a right of way. Stay on the farm road and pass some farm buildings on your left.

15. After about 300 yards, and just before the farmhouse, follow the sign to bear right then left, passing the farmhouse and its wall immediately on your left. Walk ahead along the metalled track, first between two fields then through another field. Where the track bears sharp right, leave it to walk ahead towards the woodland at the far side of the facing field. At the corner, bear right and walk with the wood on your left.

16. After a little way you will see a stile and footpath sign on your left, leading into the wood. Turn left here, go over the stile then descend bearing right along an attractive short path through the wood. Cross over a stream then leave the wooded area and continue across part of a field to go over a stile which is directly ahead. Walk ahead again with the hedge to your left until you see the footpath sign indicating a stile on your left.

17. Turn left to cross the stile then turn immediately right to join a track. You soon go through a metal gate which is by a field gate across this track and in a little over 50 yards after leaving the field you will return to where you joined the canal. Continue ahead under the bridge to reach the green in Little Bollington and your car.

Depending on the time of your return, you may wish to take the path past the pub, to visit Dunham Massey, if you have not done so on Walk 5.

Hospital for canal horses

At the far side of the canal just before Agden Underbridge, there is a building which was originally a hospital for canal horses. Even though part of the warehouse has been converted into a private house, you can still see the winch and entrance for horses on the canal side of the building.

Lloyd Bridge

This was formerly known as Outrightington Bridge but was renamed after the Lloyd Family who worked on the Bridgewater Canal for a number of generations.

Lymm

Lymm is a very attractive large village. You may wish to stop here to have a drink, a bite to eat, or simply soak up the atmosphere. Just before the bridge in the centre of the village there is a path leading up to the right to Lymm Dam, which is another pleasant spot to walk round and visit if you have the time. The dam was built to carry the A56 turnpike road over a sharp ravine, and created a lake in the process.

Lymm Cross

Lymm Cross dates from the mid-17th century, and is one of only a few similar crosses left in the country. It was constructed in sandstone on a natural red sandstone outcrop and was restored in 1897 to mark Queen Victoria's Diamond Jubilee. Even though the original purpose of the cross is unknown, it has been Grade 1 listed by English Heritage.

Lymm Cross

Places you may wish to stop for refreshment

The Swan with Two Nicks, Little Bollington: 0161 928 2914
www.swanwithtwonicks.co.uk
See Walk 5

There are also a number of pubs and very pleasant coffee shops in Lymm

The following pubs are not on the walk, but are on or near the A56 and can be reached easily by car:
The Old Number Three, Lymm Road (A56), Little Bollington
This pub was called The Old Number Three as apparently it was once the third stop for the Chester Flier passenger boats which travelled between Manchester and Chester. It is closed at present but hopefully will reopen again in the future.
The Barn Owl Inn, Agden Wharf (just off the A56) 01925 752020
www.thebarnowlinn.co.uk

WALK 7
Lymm to Grappenhall

Lymm – The Bridgewater Canal – Grappenhall – The Trans Pennine Trail – Lymm

Starting point	**The Rangers Hut adjacent to The Trans Pennine Trail in Lymm. Grid reference: 679876**
Length	**6½ miles**
Allow	**2-2½ hours**
Map	**OS Explorer 276**
By car	**Turn north off the A56 into Brookfield Road, just west of the Lymm Dam, going towards the centre of Lymm. Continue across a mini roundabout, cross the canal, and turn almost immediately left at a crossroads into Whitbarrow Road. An interesting redbrick building is on the near right corner. Go down Whitbarrow Road and in 220 yards take the first left into Statham Avenue. On your right is a small car park. Park here, or if it is full, park nearby on the road**

This walk is relatively straightforward because apart from a short suburban section around Grappenhall Village, the rest is made up of two almost equal length paths - the slightly longer Bridgewater Canal towpath and the return along The Trans Pennine Trail. Both of these are through attractive countryside, especially the latter half of the canal. It is fast, easy walking along footpaths and on reasonable all weather terrain, so you probably only need stout shoes rather than walking boots.

The Walk

1. From the car park, which is on the site of the old *Lymm Station*, return to Statham Avenue and turn left. Almost immediately turn right to retrace your steps up Whitbarrow Road. When you reach the offset crossroads in

just under 250 yards, continue ahead in the same direction, keeping the redbrick building on your right.

2. Walk down a narrower Whitbarrow Road for approximately 150 yards, and immediately after passing The Bridgewater Club on your right, cut through on your right to the canal towpath. This is before the road passes under the canal bridge. If you wish to go into *Lymm*, simply continue under the canal bridge to reach the village centre.

3. Turn right onto the canal bank and with the water on your left, you will walk along the Bridgewater Canal for almost 3 miles to leave at bridge 17, Grappenhall Bridge. For the first half mile or so it is built up with an interesting mix of old and new, both council and private houses. However the trees and curved banks give it an attractive feel. As you progress, the sound of the nearby M6 will become more prominent.

4. After almost a mile, pass under the A56 and from then onwards the surroundings become more rural, although at the same time the

The canal between Lymm and Grappenhall

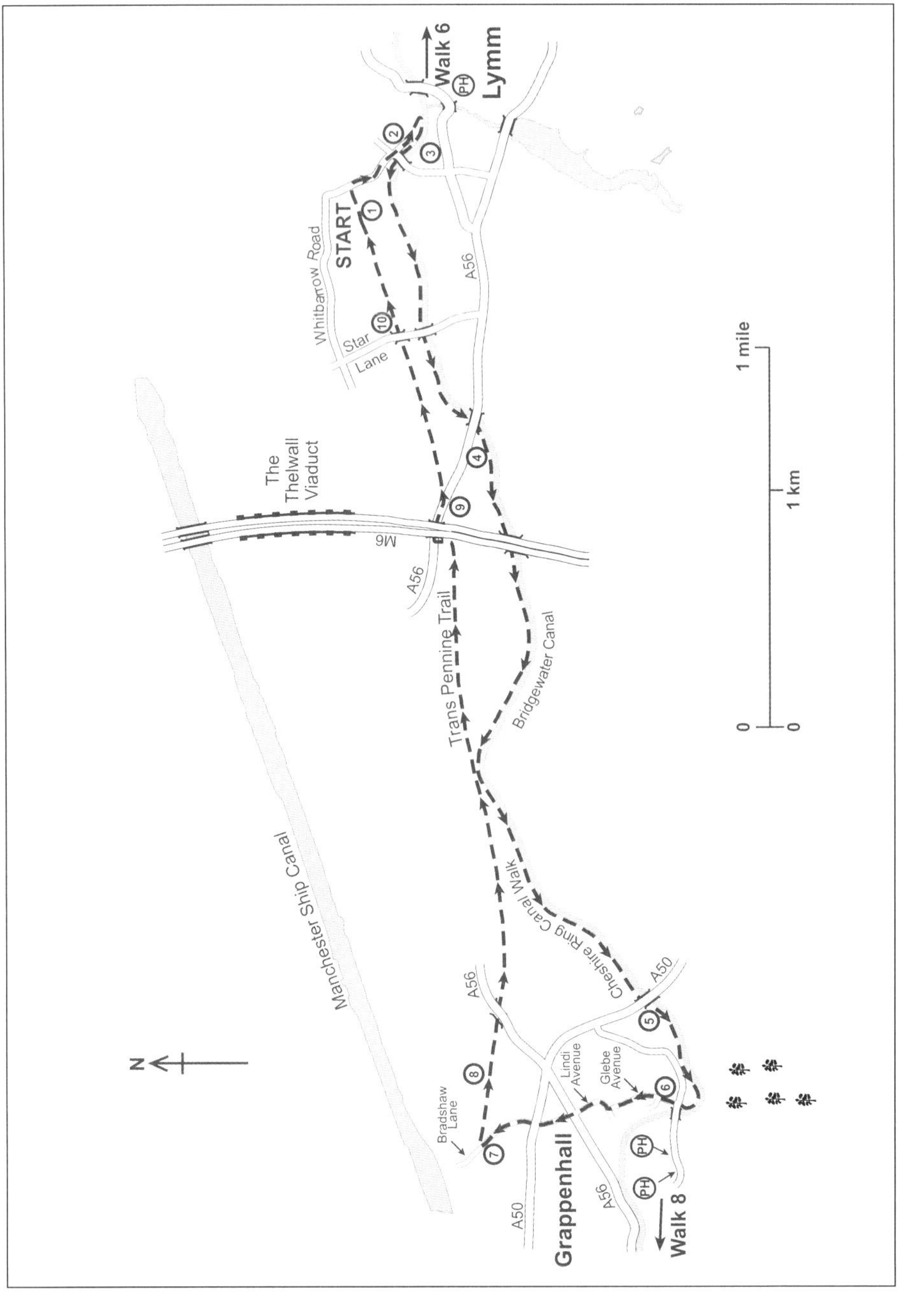

Walk 6
Lymm
PH
START
Whitbarrow Road
Star
Lane
A56
The Thelwall Viaduct
M6
Trans Pennine Trail
Bridgewater Canal
Manchester Ship Canal
Cheshire Ring Canal Walk
A50
N
Lindi Avenue
Glebe Avenue
Bradshaw Lane
Grappenhall
Walk 8
0
1 km
1 mile

motorway noise becomes louder. If you look carefully, you can see the *Thelwall Viaduct* through trees ahead to your right. Once under the M6 motorway, continue through pleasant countryside for about 1½ miles before reaching bridge 18 carrying the A50.

5. When you have passed under the A50 you will notice the section of path is especially wide and well maintained. The canal bends sharply to the right with an attractive modern development on the inside of the bend. Soon after this and just before bridge 17, the next bridge, turn right up some steps to reach the road. If you feel in need of a rest or sustenance, turn left over the bridge to the attractive centre of *Grappenhall Village* where there are two pubs which cater for all tastes.

The canal towpath near Grappenhall

6. To continue the walk, once off the canal, turn right, away from *Grappenhall Village*, and immediately left into Glebe Avenue. Walk up Glebe Avenue for about 350 yards and at the end turn right into Lindi Avenue which bends to the left and in about 150 yards takes you to Chester Road. Cross the main road and continue along East View which is straight ahead of you. After just over 150 yards you come to the A50, Knutsford Road. Here you will find a small Tesco and a fish and chip shop if you are hungry at this point. Cross the A50 and continue down Bradshaw Lane.

7. After approximately 300 yards go under a railway bridge, then take the path to your right which leads up onto the *Trans Pennine Trail.* If you have completed Walk 5, you will have walked along part of the Trans Pennine Trail before.

8. Continue along this path for approximately 2½ miles back to Lymm. It is a wide well maintained footpath, but watch out for energetic joggers, cyclists and horses! The first ⅓ mile before you come to the A50 is tree lined. About 1½ miles after joining the Trans Pennine Trail you get a clear view of *The Thelwall Viaduct* ahead to your left. Soon after the viaduct comes into view, the path turns a sharp left then right and you walk alongside the A56 to pass under the M6 again.

9. Once under the motorway, dip down to go under a low bridge carrying the A56. It is so low that horse riders are asked to dismount.

10. About ½ mile further on cross another road, with *The Star Inn* on your left. Continue along the Trail and soon the surroundings become more suburban, with modern houses and bungalows to either side. In just under ½ mile after crossing the road, you come to the Rangers hut where you leave the footpath to return to the car park and your car.

Lymm Station

Lymm station, which was on The Stockport to Warrington Line, opened in November 1853 and closed in September 1962. There is now a Rangers hut and a Trans Pennine Trail car park on the station site.

Lymm

See walk 6.

The Thelwall Viaduct

The Thelwall Viaduct carries the M6 not only over the Manchester Ship Canal, but also over the old Mersey and Irwell Navigation, a railway line and a road. Despite the building of a fourth lane, long queues can still build up here on the motorway at busy times.

Grappenhall Village

The old centre of Grappenhall Village is attractive, with a cobbled street, a church, two pubs and stocks.

The Trans Pennine Trail

See walk 5.

Places you may wish to stop for refreshment

The Ram's Head Inn, Grappenhall: *01925 269320*
www.ramsheadgrappenhall.com
Good service and good food served throughout the day (but check).
The Parr Arms, Grappenhall: *01925 212120*
The Star Inn, Lymm: *01925 753715*

There are also a number of pubs, restaurants and very pleasant coffee shops in Lymm.

WALK 8
Grappenhall to Stockton Heath

Grappenhall – The Bridgewater Canal -Stockton Heath – The Dingle – Grappenhall Heyes – Grappenhall Wood – Grappenhall

Starting point	**By the canal bridge in Grappenhall. Grid reference: 641863**
Length	**4½-5 miles**
Allow	**1¾ -2 hours**
Map	**OS Explorer 276**
By car	**If coming from the M6 junction 20 or the M56 junction 9, go down the A50 towards Warrington. Take second left (after the A50 crosses over the canal) towards Grappenhall Village. Park just before the canal bridge in Grappenhall. Walk down the slope to the right of the bridge to the towpath. If travelling along the A56, when you reach the A50 traffic lights, between Stockton Heath and Lymm, turn down the A50 towards the M6. Take the first right to Grappenhall Village then follow the above instructions. If you intend to eat or drink in 'The Ram's Head' in Grappenhall after your walk, drive over the canal bridge with care, pass the church on your right and immediately after The Ram's Head Pub turn right into its large car park. To start the walk, turn left at the road and walk back through the village to the canal. Walk over the pedestrian bridge, and left down the slope to the towpath**

This walk can divided into three parts. Firstly there is the canal section which is followed by residential Stockton Heath. The latter part of the walk through The Dingle, Grappenhall Heys and Grappenhall Wood is especially delightful. It is a relatively quick, short walk, with the possibility of a coffee stop half way round, although be prepared for mud along some of the paths after wet weather.

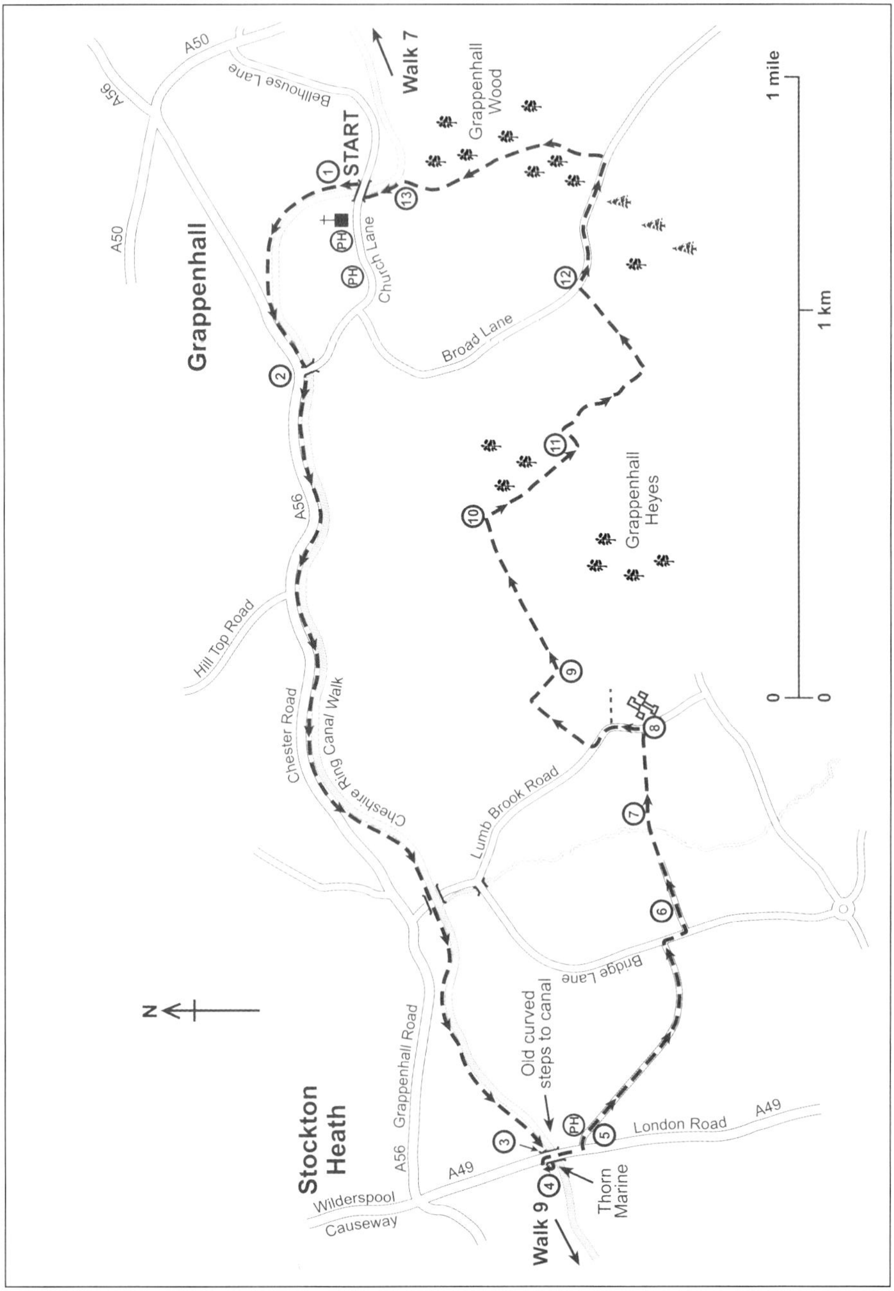

Grappenhall
START
Walk 7
Grappenhall Wood
Bellhouse Lane
A50
A56
Church Lane
PH
Broad Lane
A56
Hill Top Road
Chester Road
Cheshire Ring Canal Walk
Lumb Brook Road
Grappenhall Heyes
Bridge Lane
Grappenhall Road
Old curved steps to canal
Stockton Heath
London Road
A49
Wilderspool
Causeway
Thorn Marine
Walk 9
N
1 mile
1 km
0

The Walk

1. Go down the slope to the towpath and continue ahead. You will walk with the water to your left for almost 2 miles to leave the canal at Stockton Heath after passing under Bridge 15, the A49 London Bridge. The towpath can be muddy after rain.

2. After just under ½ mile walk under Stanney Lunt Bridge and less than a mile after this, cross Lumb Brook Road Underbridge. This section of the canal between the two bridges runs parallel to the A56 and can be noisy at times. Coming towards the outskirts of Stockton Heath you walk behind the backs of houses before passing a small marina followed by the London Bridge Pub on the far side of the canal. Note the *curved steps* in the pub grounds, which lead down to the canal. Here people used to disembark from the original passenger *packet boat and fly boat services* which once plied along the canal. You can see the old stable buildings and smithy behind the steps to the left.

Steps once used by packet boat passengers, with old stables behind

3. Walk under the imposing London Bridge which carries the A49, followed by the old buildings housing *Thorn Marine Chandlery* on your right. It is thought that the old *Stockton Quay* was opposite here, although it is difficult to find its exact location and it may have been the other side of the A49 bridge. Immediately after the chandlery turn right to reach Mitchell Street. Redevelopment has been talked about so there may be other buildings on the site of the chandlery in the future.

Thorn Marine Chandlery, Stockton Heath

4. Turn right onto Mitchell Street, then right again onto the A49. If you wish to go into Stockton Heath, turn left onto the A49 where you will find shops, cafés/restaurants and pubs. However, to continue the walk, cross the main road at the crossing, and turn right, passing over the canal to reach the *London Bridge Pub* on your left.

5. In less than 50 yards after the pub car park entrance, turn left into Dingleway. It is signposted, on the far side of the main road, to St Monica's RC Primary School and Broomfields Leisure Centre. Dingleway bears to the right and you continue along here for just over $\frac{1}{3}$ mile, eventually bearing to the left past St Monica's RC Primary School on your right, to reach a T-junction. Here you turn right onto Bridge Lane. Walk past St Mary Magdalene's Church. Cross the road, continue in the same direction and almost immediately there is a narrow footpath going down between houses on your left, which you take.

6. This footpath leads you down between houses and bungalows to a small parking area on your right. Continue ahead here, keeping to the left of a row of 'modern' terraces, and this will take you down to Dale Lane at the bottom. At the lane, turn left then almost immediately right across a small bridge over a brook. This area is known as The Dingle. You have now joined the Mersey Valley Way which you will follow all the way, with twists and turns, back to Grappenhall.

7. Once over the brook, continue in the same direction, gradually climbing. Where a path crosses, do not take the wider left hand track, but continue ahead. The footpath takes you across private land on either side to reach Lumb Brook Road in just over 300 yards after leaving Dale Lane.

8. Cross the road onto a pavement. Turn left. Ignore the first path to your right, which is beside a gate house. The road bears left, and about 170 yards after leaving the footpath you will see a small wooded area and a footpath sign to the right, directing you to *Grappenhall Village*. Turn right here. Go through a metal kissing gate onto a wide path which continues straight ahead through a narrow strip of mature woodland for about 200 yards, before bearing right.

9. Continue along here for about 100 yards before the path bears left just before a field ahead, though this may be built on in the future. Continue with the field on your right for a short while followed by the houses of *Grappenhall Heyes*, also on your right.

10. As the houses end, turn right with the houses still on your right. Continue through the copse and where the paths diverge continue to keep right. Go down some steps and over a small bridge with a pool to your left. Carry on in the same direction to the end of the pleasant woodland.

11. Go through a gate, turn left along a track, and then almost immediately right to walk along a wide sandy path with relatively young woodland to either side. After just under 300 yards and at the end of this path, pass over a small bridge and turn left to follow a sign towards 'Grappenhall Wood'. Continue along here for about 300 yards to reach Broad Lane.

Grappenhall Wood

12. Turn right onto Broad Lane and after just under 400 yards and before you reach the building, turn left into Grappenhall Wood, which is owned by the Woodland Trust. Walk ahead here away from the road for about ¼ mile. Initially keep towards the right of the light woodland and don't take

any of the left hand paths. When the main path appears to diverge in a clearing, bear left towards a footpath sign ahead. Continue on this path.

13. At the far end of Grappenhall Wood go through a metal gate and walk along an enclosed pathway, until you reach the canal ahead. Here you turn left and in just under 100 yards you will return to the bridge in *Grappenhall Village* and to your car.

Grappenhall Village and church

Grappenhall Village

See walk 7.

Steps leading to The London Bridge Pub

When the canals were used for commercial and passenger transport, passenger packet and fly boats would stop at the curved steps adjacent to the pub for a change of horses and to allow people to embark and disembark. The Duchess-Countess was the most well known of the boats which stopped at the steps next to the pub between the 1770s and the mid 1880s. Most of the original canal side buildings have disappeared, although behind the pub the smithy and stables can still be seen.

Packet boats and fly boats

See walk 4.

Stockton Quay

Stockton Quay was the terminus of the canal from 1769 to 1772 before the route from Worsley and Manchester was finally completed through to Preston Brook and Runcorn. As a result it developed as a major trans- shipment quay with wharves, canal company offices, yards, stables and warehouses and also Cash's Boat Yard. The quay continued to flourish throughout the heyday of the canal. Any remaining warehouses and the boatyard were demolished in the mid 1980s.

Thorn Marine Chandlery

Thorn Marine occupies buildings which were originally stables and staff houses for canal workers, and part of it was also used as a fodder store. The furthest side of the shop from the A49 used to be the Lancashire Constabulary and also the canal mortuary. The mortuary was in use until 1951, the tiles of which can still be seen. Unfortunately there are plans to demolish Thorne Marine, so at some point in the future, housing may be in its place. But as the current shop tenants have had the demolition threat hanging over their heads for over 7 years, there is hope this may not happen for a while.

Grappenhall Heyes

The new houses of Grappenhall Heyes are on the land once occupied by Grappenhall Hall, home of The Parr family, which was destroyed by fire in the 1970s. The surrounding land now belongs to the Woodland Trust.

Places you may wish to stop for refreshment

The Ram's Head Inn, Grappenhall: *01925 269320*
www.ramsheadgrappenhall.com
Good service and good food served throughout the day (but check).
The Parr Arms, Grappenhall: *01925 212120*
The London Bridge Pub, Stockton Heath: *01925 267904. A pleasant welcoming atmosphere. An ideal coffee stop with good value food and drink.*

There are a number of coffee shops, pubs and restaurants in Stockton Heath.

WALK 9
Stockton Heath to Moore

Stockton Heath – The Bridgewater Canal – Moore – Appleton Reservoir – Walton Hall Golf Course – Stockton Heath

Starting point	**Mitchell Street off the A49 in Stockton Heath, Warrington. Grid reference: 615858**
Length	**7 miles**
Allow	**2¾-3 hours**
Map	**OS Explorer 276**
By car	**From the M56 Junction 10, take the A49 north towards Stockton Heath and Warrington. After approximately 2½ miles and with the London Bridge Pub on your right, cross the canal bridge and turn immediate left down Mitchell Street. Park as near to the junction as you can. If this is not possible, continue down Mitchell Street, bear left at the end and park somewhere close to the canal, or on one of the streets nearby. If you do this, start the walk from where you park and complete the last short canal stretch from the bridge to your car, at the end of the walk. If coming from the A56, or Warrington, when you reach Stockton Heath, take the A49 south towards the M56. Immediately before the canal bridge turn right into Mitchell Street. Then follow the above instructions**

This is one of the longest walks in the book, but it is a very pleasant one and because it is varied and mainly rural, the time passes quickly. The canal is tree lined in parts, and runs alongside Walton Gardens. The return section includes field paths, an attractive stretch around Appleton Reservoir and a longer path across Walton Hall Golf Club.

The Walk

1. From Mitchell Street, go through the gap in the buildings by *Thorn Marine Chandlery* to reach the towpath of The Bridgewater Canal. Opposite is possibly the site of the former *Stockton Quay*. Turn right. You will walk with the water on your left for approximately 2½ miles until you leave at Bridge 7 in Moore. The first stretch of towpath is suburban but soon becomes rural, and after walking under Hough's bridge, the canal passes through a cutting with woodland at either side.

Hough's Bridge

2. You soon walk under Walton Lea Bridge, and the newer metal pedestrian bridge alongside it. Come off the canal here if you wish to visit *Walton Gardens*, the *café at Walton Gardens*, or *the Walton Arms.* Note the rhododendrons along this stretch of canal which are glorious in late spring. Just under ½ mile after Walton Lea Bridge you walk under the 'toast rack' bridge, carrying the A56.

The 'toast rack' bridge carrying the A56

3. Almost a mile after passing under the A56 you reach *Moore.* Walk under the bridge and go a few more yards before leaving the canal to your right. You may of course leave the towpath earlier if you wish to visit the small shop facing the canal and then continue along the road to the bridge over the canal. However, if you plan to truly walk the whole of The Cheshire Ring you would then have to return to where you have left the towpath, when you start Walk 10!

4. Walk over the canal bridge into Hobb Lane which you climb gradually for about ½ mile to reach the A56. This lane is quiet, but is narrow and

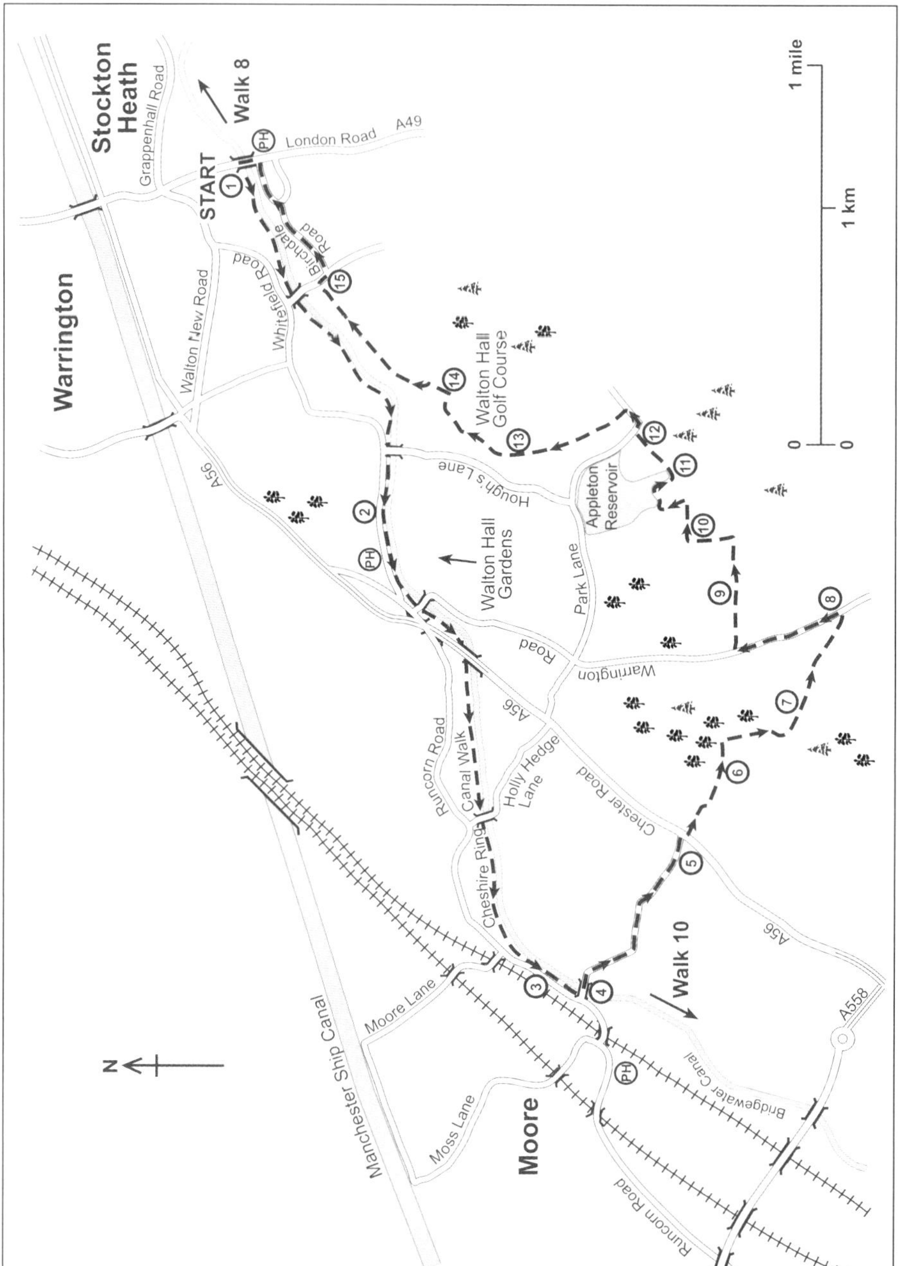
Stockton Heath
Warrington
Moore
Walk 8
Walk 10
START
Grappenhall Road
London Road
A49
PH
Walton New Road
Whitefield Road
Birchdale Road
Walton Hall Golf Course
Hough's Lane
Appleton Reservoir
Park Lane
Walton Hall Gardens
Warrington Road
A56
Runcorn Road
Canal Walk
Holly Hedge Lane
Chester Road
Cheshire Ring
Moore Lane
Moss Lane
Manchester Ship Canal
Bridgewater Canal
A558
N
1 mile
1 km
0
0
1
2
3
4
5
6
7
8
9
10
11
12
13
14
15

twisty, so stay vigilant and look out for the occasional car. There are a number of imposing houses to your right with even more imposing gates and walls. You can see the *Daresbury Science and Innovation Centre* Tower through a gap between buildings on your right.

View of Daresbury Science and Innovation Centre from Hobb Lane

5. At the A56 take the diagonal path on your right to the roadside, then cross the busy road with care. Ahead is a gate with a footpath sign, which you follow. Continue in same direction for just over 150 yards. At the edge of a small copse on the right you will notice a sign on the right indicating footpaths to the right and ahead left. Go ahead left following an unclear but discernable path across a large field to the corner of Row's Wood ahead. At the time of writing pipes were being laid in a field nearby so there is a possibility that the field layout may be changing. However, the footpath should still be there.

6. When you're almost at the corner of the wood, go through a gate then keep ahead right so you are walking round the field with the wood (in which you may well see bamboo being cultivated) to your left. Turn right at the corner of the field, still keeping the wood to your left and the field to your right. In 200-250 yards, go through a gate on your left, and walk ahead right on a path that cuts to the other side of the wood.

7. When you leave the wood, continue ahead keeping the trees, a ditch and edge of the field directly on your right. Do not be tempted to bear left. At the far side of the field, turn left for a few yards along the far hedge then turn right through a gate to continue in the original direction. Walk ahead through the next field keeping parallel to a wavy hedge on your left. At the far end of this field, go through another gate which is on the left. Turn left across the next small field then through the gate to the left of two trees, to reach Warrington Road.

8. Turn left onto Warrington Road and continue for about ⅓ mile. Take the first footpath on your right to go over a stile by a gate. It is signposted to 'The Mersey Valley Trail'. You will follow this trail – which later becomes 'The Delamere Way' – to almost the end of the walk, although it is not a straight path, not always well signposted and not always clear!

9. Keep the field boundary on your right and walk through two fields. Cross a farm track, then go ahead into another field and just before reaching the wood turn left. You will now walk with the wood on your right. Ignore the first 'corner' stile into the wood, and continue ahead, then just before the end of the field go over a short bridge to your right followed by a stile. This will lead you to a wide path which goes through the wood.

10. Walk through the wood and just before you emerge into the open at the far side, turn left, so you are still in the wood. Walk a little way and you will soon come to a stile on your right. Turn right to cross the stile and walk ahead along a type of footbridge keeping Appleton Reservoir to your left. Walk along a path which bears right and becomes raised, then climb a few steps to reach a narrow lane.

11. Turn left at the lane and continue ahead, ignoring the footpath to the left which takes you around the edge of the reservoir. After just over 250 yards you reach Park Lane. However, if you wish to walk around part of the reservoir, take that footpath to the left and simply reach Park Lane by a slightly longer route.

12. Turn right onto Park Lane, which almost at once bears to the left. Immediately after the dwellings on your left, you will see a footpath sign and gate, also on your left. Go through the gate onto Walton Hall Golf Course. Walk through Walton Hall Golf Course for about ½ mile. Here you must keep left so you walk ahead alongside a small stream. You need to follow the signs and also the white posts.

13. After a while the stream bears right and you cross over a small bridge on your left. Continue to follow the footpath signs, to eventually reach a sandy path. Turn right, dip down, then immediately leave the path to cross a stile which is up to your left. Once you are off the golf course, turn right to go in the direction of Stockton Heath.

14. This takes you along a bridleway for a little over ½ mile. Where there is a

Appleton Reservoir

footpath signposted up the hill to the right, do not take it, but continue ahead. The bridleway bears slightly left then right to go through a courtyard and past a number of barn conversions. Continue ahead on the track.

15. When you reach Red Lane about ⅓ mile after the courtyard, turn right then take the first left down Birchdale Road. Walk along Birchdale Road, passing a variety of old and new houses, and in less than ½ mile you come out onto the A56 opposite the *London Bridge Pub*. Turn left, go over the canal bridge, and take an immediate left again into Mitchell Street to return to your car.

Thorn Marine Chandlery

See walk 8.

Stockton Quay

See Walk 8.

Walton Gardens

These gardens were bought by Warrington Borough Council in 1941 and they have been a public park since 1945. There is a small zoo here which is popular with young children.

Moore

This is an attractive canal side village with moorings, and a village shop. You would not know it was so close to Runcorn.

Daresbury Science and Innovation Centre

See walk 10.

Places you may wish to stop for refreshment

Café in Walton Gardens
The Watlon Arms Pub: *01925 262659. A family orientated pub at the end of the drive to Walton Gardens.*
The London Bridge Pub, Stockton Heath: *01925 267904. See walk 8.*

WALK 10

Moore to Preston Brook

Moore – The Bridgewater Canal – Preston Brook – Marine Village – The Runcorn Branch of the Bridgewater Canal – Red Brow – Daresbury Firs/Keckwick Hill – Moore

Starting point	**Moore, south west of Warrington. Grid reference: 578843**
Length	**6½-7 miles**
Allow	**2½-3hours**
Maps	**OS Explorer 276 and OS Explorer 267**
By car	**From the M56 Junction 11, take the A56 north towards Warrington. Keep ahead right past the A558 Daresbury Expressway junction. Just under a mile later turn left down the narrow Hobb Lane to Moore. Cross the canal bridge in Moore and turn left. The road bends sharp right, crosses a railway bridge then bends left again. Park on the left near the Red Lion Inn, or if you wish to visit there afterwards, park in their car park**

This is the last of the Bridgewater Canal walks! The canal section passes the well designed Daresbury Science and Innovation Centre at Keckwick and there are far reaching views from much of the towpath. The return, which crosses the canal twice, is very varied, and includes Murdishaw Valley, Marine Village, a short section along The Runcorn Branch, good open views and Daresbury Firs and Keckwick Hill.

The Walk

1. Walk back to the canal bridge in Moore.

2. Turn right onto the towpath then right again. You will walk with the water to your left for just over 2½ miles until you leave at Bridge 1, Preston

Brook. There are four interesting information boards along this part of the canal. The first is found at the start, followed by boards near the science park, by the bridge over the Runcorn Arm and at Preston Brook. It is suggested you take time to read them. In just under a mile walk under the A558, followed by the narrower *Keckwick Bridge.*

3. Once past the A558 bridge you will see the renowned *Daresbury Science and Innovation Centre* on your left. The large science centre fits well into its setting, and is well landscaped, especially along the canal bank. You can see the striking tower from miles around. Continue along the towpath. There are some glorious views along this section. To your right you can see the Fiddlers Ferry Power Station and the Halton Water Tower, and on a clear day, if you turn round you can see the Winter Hill radio mast on Rivington Moor to the north beyond Bolton.

4. In just under 2½ miles after joining the canal you come to its junction with the Runcorn Branch of the Bridgewater Canal. Cross this and continue in the same direction to pass under the busy M56. The towpath

Looking back along the canal towpath before reaching the Runcorn Branch

now widens to become a road and as you approach *Preston Brook* note the moored boats and the chandlers shop on the opposite bank. Follow the road up past some attractive former canal workers' cottages, and at the top, join the A56 at *Preston Brook.*

Looking towards the A56 at Preston Brook

5. When you reach the main road, turn right and walk along the A56, passing a shop on your left. After about 200 yards, turn right into Gorseywell Lane, then immediately left into Sandy Lane. Walk along Sandy Lane for just over 200 yards, keeping right when Aston Green joins from the left. At what seems to be a 'dead end' (but isn't!) turn left to climb and cross a footbridge over the M56.

Old canal workers' cottages at Preston Brook

6. Once over the motorway, continue in the same direction through a wooded area and in under 100 yards where a path joins from the left, bear right. You are now in Murdishaw Valley, a local nature reserve. You will see some steps up to your left leading to houses, do not take these. Just past the steps, a lesser path joins from the right which you do not take either but continue along the main path which runs parallel to the houses up behind the trees on your left. You soon come to Marine Lane.

7. At the road turn right and then take the first left into Marine Village. Walk through this attractive canal side development, keeping largely in the same direction. The road soon bears left then right, in front of a small square. After the square, take the first right, which leads you past some

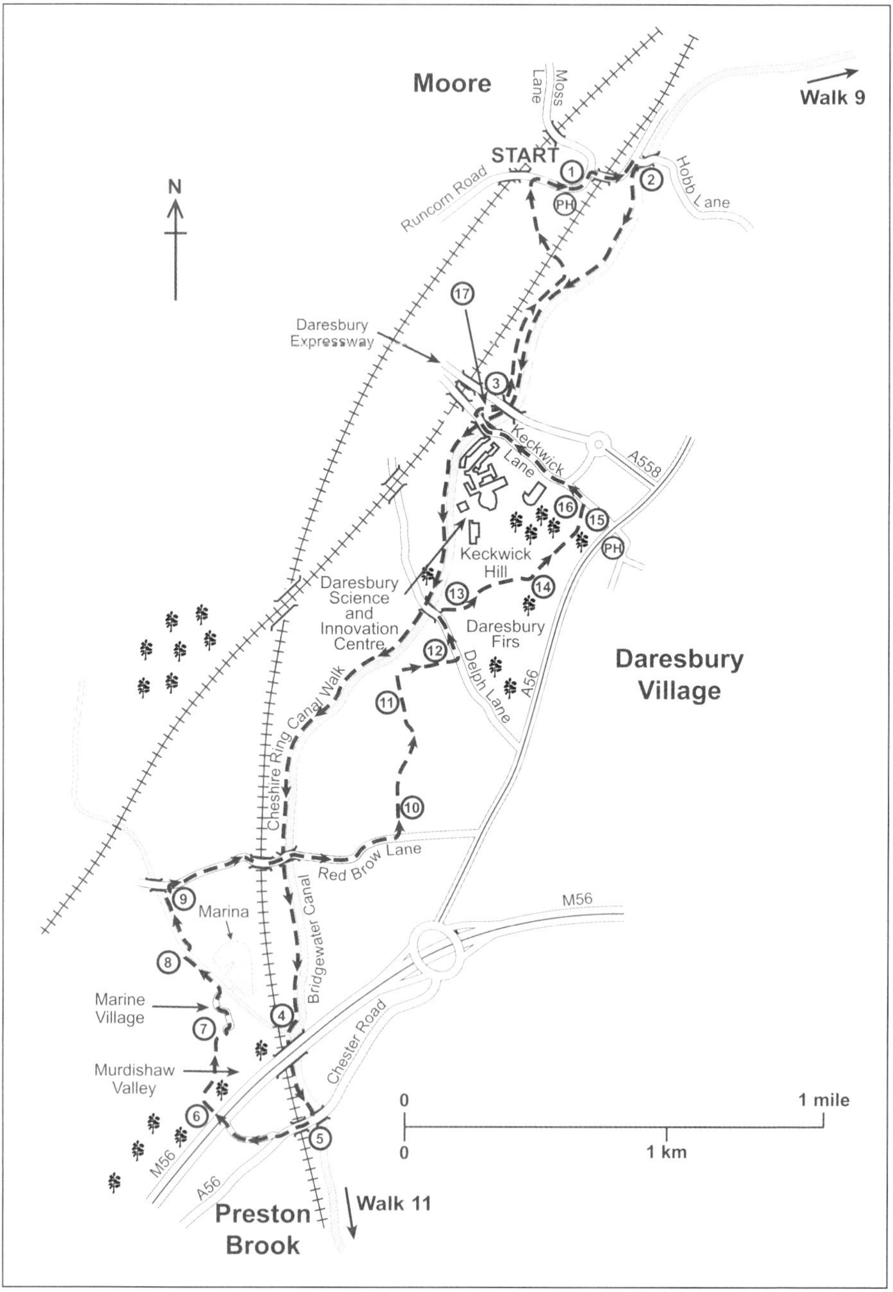
Moore
Moss Lane
Walk 9
START
Runcorn Road
Hobb Lane
PH
N
Daresbury Expressway
Keckwick Lane
A558
Keckwick Hill
Daresbury Science and Innovation Centre
Daresbury Firs
Delph Lane
A56
Daresbury Village
Cheshire Ring Canal Walk
Red Brow Lane
Bridgewater Canal
Marina
M56
Marine Village
Murdishaw Valley
Chester Road
0
1 mile
0
1 km
Preston Brook
Walk 11

garages to the bank of the Runcorn Branch of the Bridgewater Canal. At the canal turn left. Note *Preston Brook Marina* on the far side of the canal. Walk along the canal for about 200 yards and just before a willow tree, the path bears to the left and leads you back to Marine Lane.

8. Turn right, and walk along Marine Lane for less than 50 yards before turning right onto a wide metalled path which takes you over the canal. There is a sign to 'The Marina'. Once over the canal, turn left and walk with the water on your left for about 300 yards until you reach a bridge.

9. Turn right just before the bridge, and right again onto Red Brow Lane. The lane descends to reach the main Liverpool to London Railway line which you will walk across. Take great care, and make sure you observe the green and red lights. Once across the railway line, the road climbs steeply. Walk under the canal in a steep cutting and continue to climb. In slightly over ¼ mile after the road passes under the canal, and before you reach another road ahead, there is a footpath sign on your left. This is just after the brow of the hill and opposite office buildings on your right. Note that an expansion of Daresbury Business Park has been proposed, so in the future there may be some slight changes to the layout of Red Brow Lane and the following footpaths. It is hoped that these changes, if made, will only be minor.

10. Turn left at the stile and contour the hillside on a path which is initially between two fences. After this, cross a stile, and continue in the same direction. The Business Park is to your right and to your left there are good views towards the canal and beyond. At the end of the field, go a few yards to the left to cross over another stile. Keeping ahead, make for a gap between a farmhouse and large old barn which you will see lower down at the far side of the field.

11. Walk between the farm house and barn then turn right, and keeping the barn on your right, walk along a driveway. After about 200 yards you come to Delph Lane. Note the line of impressive houses ahead, all which probably have good views.

12. Turn left at Delph Lane and walk past a number of houses on your right, noting the far reaching views to your left. In about 200 yards - before reaching the canal bridge and just past the last house on your right - you will see a large gap by a gate on your right.

13. Turn right here and walk up to *Daresbury Firs and Keckwick Hill.* Keep to the right whilst walking up the first field. Go through a gate into Daresbury Firs. Once through the gate, you may wish to look at the plan of the woods on your left. There are two paths ahead, take the main left hand one, keeping the 'Daresbury Firs' sign to your right. Ignore a minor path which joins on your left and continue ahead gradually climbing, ignoring another path which crosses a little further on.

14. Eventually you come to the top and far side of the woods, with a map and 'Daresbury Firs' sign on your right. Here you bear forward left on an unclear path. You need to walk just to the right of the bench and post, but to the left of the Daresbury Firs exit ahead. Walk along inside the woods, keeping the field to your right. The path is unclear but you should not go wrong if you keep reasonably close to the edge of the woods, until you bear left down a few shallow steps - but you must look out for them! Now walk ahead a few steps. Turn right, then bear left by a large tree root, keeping the boundary and outside field corner behind you. Walk to the right of a tree trunk ahead which has branches part of the way up but no top, then keep ahead right on the flat, making sure you don't veer down towards the left. The path becomes clearer and you may see the tower of the Science Park down through the trees to your left. If in doubt, keep largely to the right!

15. Soon after a 'Danger Cliff Face' sigh on the right, you can see new buildings of the Science Park in the near distance. Slowly descend, keeping largely in the same direction and pass some boards with information down to your right . You are making for metal bars ahead of you which indicate a more enclosed footpath out of Daresbury Firs. Walk down this footpath to Keckwick Lane. *The Ring o'Bells* in Daresbury is about ¼ mile from here to your right.

16. Turn left and walk down Keckwick Lane for 100 yards to reach a roundabout. Go over the roundabout and continue ahead along a road which takes you through part of Daresbury Science and Innovation Centre. Pass a number of impressive buildings in this ever expanding science park. In just under ¼ mile after the roundabout, cross over the Bridgewater Canal, and walk down to the left onto the towpath.

17. Turn left along the towpath to walk with the water on your right for just over ⅓ mile. Pass under Keckwick Lane followed almost immediately by

the Daresbury Expressway then leave the towpath at the next footbridge. Continue along a track in the same direction for a few more yards before bearing left as it turns away from the water. This takes you over a railway line and past a path which joins from the left. About ⅓ mile after leaving the canal you come to Runcorn Lane. Turn right to reach The Red Lion Public House and return to your car.

Moore

See Walk 9.

Keckwick Bridge and Daresbury Village

Daresbury, about half a mile from Keckwick Bridge, is the birthplace of Charles Dodgson, better known as Lewis Carroll the creator of 'Alice in Wonderland'. In the church there, you can see the characters from the book depicted in one of the stained glass windows. Charles Dodgson's father was the Vicar of Daresbury. He was interested in the lives of the local bargemen, and provided a floating chapel near Keckwick Bridge for them to hold services. This was apparently well used by the people who worked on the canal.

Daresbury Science and Innovation Centre

The iconic tower belonging to this building was originally part of a Vertical Particle Accelerator, or Van de Graaff Generator, but it is no longer used for this and has now been assimilated into the larger laboratory. On the same site is 'The Synchotron', one of the largest units for the research of particle physics in the country. The laboratories fit surprisingly well into the local landscape.

Preston Brook, and Preston Brook Marina

The village grew up around the canal. At one time it was a bustling wharf and one of the busiest canal centres in the North West. Until the end of the Second World War goods were transferred here from the wider boats from The River Mersey to the narrow canal boats of The Midlands and visa versa. Unfortunately all the warehouses connected to this activity have now been demolished although you can still see the cottages which were built to house the workers on the right of the towpath just before the A56.

Commercial traffic stopped on the canal in 1974 but at around the same time, Preston Brook Marina opened with moorings for 300 pleasure boats. Marine Village was built opposite the marina and now the area is bustling with leisure craft. In 2005 The National Waterways Festival was held at Preston Brook.

Daresbury Firs and Keckwick Hill

There was originally a woodland here in the 19th century but much of this was cut down at the beginning of the 20th century. The present pines were planted in 1978 to be used commercially, but in 1996 the Firs and Hill were bought by Halton Borough Council. Groundwork Mersey Valley now helps manage the area as a community woodland. Both the Firs and Keckwick Hill are pleasant walking areas.

Places you may wish to stop for refreshment

The Red Lion Inn, Moore: *01925 740101*
The Ring o' Bells, Daresbury: 01925 740256, *Although not along the route of the walk, this pub serves good food all day. You may wish to look round the church opposite whilst you are here.*
www.chefandbrewer.com/pubs/cheshire/ring-o-bells

WALK 11
Preston Brook to Lodge Lane

Preston on the Hill – Preston Brook – The Bridgewater Canal – Dutton –The Trent and Mersey Canal – Lodge Lane – Marsh Lane – Preston on the Hill

Starting point	**Preston on the Hill. Grid reference: 571808**
Length	**5½ miles**
Allow	**Approximately 2½ hours**
Map	**OS Explorer 267**
By car	**From the M56 Junction 11, take the A56 south, and in less than ¼ mile turn left to Preston on the Hill. Drive into the village and park after you have passed Summer Lane on your left. You will need to pull up onto the pavement, but this is no problem as it is wide and many others do it**

You pass from The Bridgewater Canal to The Trent and Mersey Canal on this walk, though as this occurs underneath as you walk above Preston Brook Tunnel, you are unaware of it! The Preston Brook Tunnel is the first of five tunnels on The Cheshire Ring, four of which, like this one you walk over rather than through. Much of the canal is quiet and rural, especially the delightful southern parts alongside Longacre Wood. The lanes are relatively quiet and the factories around the northern section are well hidden from the surprisingly attractive (considering where it is situated) Preston on the Hill. Some of the field paths can be muddy especially after wet weather.

The Walk

1. Walk ahead, away from where you have come from. Continue for a few yards and you will see a road sloping down steeply to your right, signposted towards Chester. Walk down here for just over 300 yards to reach the A56. Turn left, cross the canal, and walk down to your left

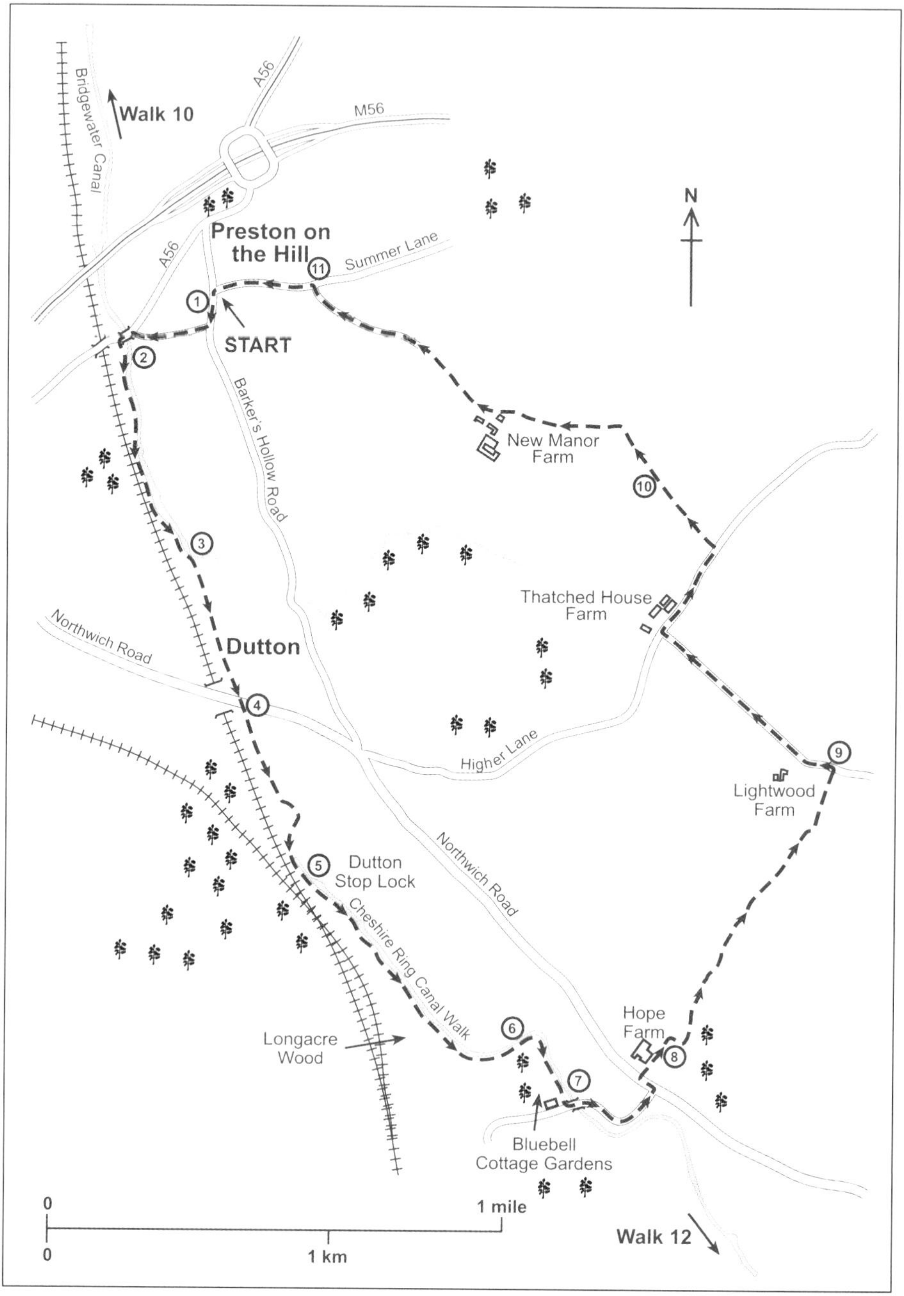
Bridgewater Canal
Walk 10
A56
M56
Preston on the Hill
A56
Summer Lane
11
1
START
2
N
Barker's Hollow Road
New Manor Farm
10
3
Thatched House Farm
Northwich Road
Dutton
4
Higher Lane
9
Lightwood Farm
5
Dutton Stop Lock
Northwich Road
Cheshire Ring Canal Walk
Hope Farm
6
8
Longacre Wood
7
Bluebell Cottage Gardens
0
1 mile
0
1 km
Walk 12

beside Canalside Cottages, to join the towpath at *Preston Brook.* You will eventually leave the canal at Lodge Lane after just over 2 miles, but for about ⅔ mile of this you will be above the water as it travels through the 1,239 yard long *Preston Brook Tunnel.*

2. Once on the towpath, turn right and walk with the water initially on your left. Walk past modern housing followed by a renovated warehouse on your left. To your right is a railway line with houses behind, but these are well shielded by trees and other foliage. The landscape soon becomes rural and will remain so for the rest of the walk.

3, After about ¾ mile you reach *Preston Brook Tunnel* and here you climb to your right and cross over above the canal. Continue in the same direction as the canal along Tunnel Top North for about ⅓ mile until you reach the A533.

Looking back at The Preston Brook Tunnel

4. From Tunnel Top North, cross the A533 with care, turn left and then almost immediately right along a British Waterways metalled pathway which is Tunnel Top South. Walk along Tunnel Top South for about ⅓ mile, noting the two air vents to your right. The path bends to the right and eventually descends once again to cross the canal. Turn left onto the canal towpath. Take care not to miss this turn which is by two white cottages.

Dry dock built by the North Staffordshire Railway Company

5. You will walk along the canal for almost a mile. Note the board telling you that you are now on the Trent and Mersey Canal. Just past this you will see *Dutton*

Stop Lock followed by *Dutton Dry Dock*. The following stretch of water is pleasant and rural. For much of the way you will walk alongside the ancient semi-natural woodland of Longacre Wood, maintained by the Woodland Trust. At the notice board you may, if you wish, turn into the wood and walk the next stretch almost parallel to the canal, keeping left by wooden posts to reach the end of the woodland. This is worth doing, especially at bluebell time. However, it means missing out on a short section of canal, so if you want to be able to say you have walked the whole canal ring, you will have to retrace your steps back to where you left the towpath, before continuing the walk!

6. Once past the woods, the canal bends to the left and after that to the right. In just under a mile after rejoining the towpath you come to bridge 213 after which you leave the canal to the right. If you wish to have a rest and short diversion, *Bluebell Cottage Gardens* are a few yards to your left from the bridge along Lodge Lane. Here there is a café, a good nursery and also gardens which you may visit, for a small fee.

The Dutton Stop Lock

7. However, if you are not stopping, turn right to cross over the canal bridge and walk along the narrow Lodge Lane which bends to the right and left. About ¼ mile after leaving the canal you reach the A533. Turn left and walk along the pavement for about 50 yards and you will see a footpath sign on your right just before some farm buildings. Cross the road with care and follow this footpath sign to walk away from the road along what is initially a farm track.

Bridge 213

8. Walk past Hope Farm on your left. After a little while the path turns a sharp right then left to continue in the same direction. Just over 300 yards after the left bend and after passing a small woodland on your right, the track becomes wider and muddier with some piles of rubble to the right. Just past here, and at the end of a short hedge on your left, go over a partly hidden stile ahead left, and continue in the same direction with a hedge now on your right. Continue ahead over several stiles, keeping parallel to the hedge or wire fence on your right and ensuring you don't veer left. In the last field, where you can see Lightwood Farm to your left, the stile is in the far right hand corner, but it is not easy to see until you are very close.

9. Turn left onto Marsh Lane and walk for just under half a mile along this quiet road. When you come to a T-junction with Thatched House Farm ahead, turn right down Higher Lane. Walk along here for ¼ mile, until you see a footpath sign and stile to your left. These are half way along a hedge and not very clear until you get to them and you will probably see another stile at the far side of this field before you see the one beside the road. At the sign turn left over the stile and walk across the field in a straight direction away from the road. Cross the second stile and keep to the left hand side of a small wood ahead.

10. Once past the woodland, cross another field with a pond on your right, and at the end of this bear left round some trees, following the signs. It can be muddy, especially after wet weather. At the second farm gate,

(usually left open) follow a footpath sign over a stile to its right, so you now walk with a hedge on your left. Immediately after a brick barn on your left, you will see a footpath sign which directs you over a stile on your left and onto a tarmac driveway. When you have crossed over the stile, turn right and walk past New Manor Farm, noting the attractive building and former moat. You now walk along the driveway for about ½ mile before reaching Summer Lane.

11. Turn left along Summer Lane and in about ¼ mile you will come to Preston on the Hill. Turn left and return to your car.

Preston Brook

See Walk 10.

Preston Brook Tunnel

The 1,239 yard long Preston Brook Tunnel is possibly best known for the fact that the junction between the Bridgewater Canal and the Trent and Mersey Canal is just inside its northern end. However you will not be walking through the tunnel but above it. When the canals were built, certain tunnels were not wide enough for towpaths, so the horses were unhitched and walked above the canal. The boats were then propelled by men who lay on their backs on cross plank, and pushed the boat by 'walking' their feet along the tunnel roof. Groups of men were employed simply to do this job. In 1865 steam tugs began to be used to pull the boats through the tunnel. However it was soon realised that ventilation was needed to get rid of the fumes, so four ventilation shafts were built.

In 1981, part of the tunnel collapsed, destroying Dutton Post Office which was never rebuilt. A new access and inspection shaft was built by the site of the crater and this, along with another ventilation shaft can be seen. The tunnel was re-opened again in 1984.

Dutton Stop Lock and Dutton Dry Dock

When you rejoin the towpath at the southern end of the tunnel, you will see a stop lock which was constructed by The Trent and Mersey Canal Company to protect their water supply. Just past this on the far side of the canal is a dry dock built by The North Staffordshire Railway Company who oversaw the running of the canal between 1846 and 1923. The dock was built for the maintenance of its tunnel tugs. Note the railway-type boarding around the dock.

Places you may wish to stop for refreshment

Bluebell Cottage Gardens and Lodge Lane Nurseries: *01928 713718* **www.bluebellcottage.co.uk** *Open mid March to the end of September (but check).*

There is a plant nursery and tearoom here plus the attractive Bluebell Cottage Gardens which can be visited for a small fee. Behind the gardens are some delightful bluebell woods. If you wish to visit these gardens at the same time as going on walks 11 or 12 you could possibly park in the car park here and do the walks, starting part way through. But check with someone first as parking is limited. If so, turn left out of the car park to start the walks. It is not possible to park on the roads nearby.

WALK 12

Lodge Lane to south of Acton Bridge

Acton Bridge – The River Weaver – Dutton Locks – Lodge Lane – The Trent and Mersey Canal – Willow Green – Acton Bridge

Starting point	**Acton Bridge, where the A49 crosses The River Weaver. Grid reference: 601761**
Length	**5 miles**
Allow	**1¾-2 hours**
Map	**OS Explorer 267**
By car	**Take the A49 south from junction 10 of the M56. After about 4 miles, and immediately before the road crosses the River Weaver, turn left towards The Leigh Arms. If you are going to the pub later, park in their large car park which backs onto the river bank or alternatively park on the road nearby. If coming from the south along the A49, the road crosses The River Weaver about 1½ miles north of the Weaverham roundabout. Turn right immediately after the swing bridge and park as above**

This is a delightful walk, especially in the springtime. It is also a very 'watery' walk! Much of the first half is along the River Weaver, and the return is along the canal. Between the two, there is a pleasant path and an attractive little woodland. If you are able to do so, go on this walk (and also walk 13) when the bluebells are out, and you will not be disappointed.

Note – In September 2012 after many months of heavy rain there was a large breach of the canal bank south of Lodge Lane. The canal and towpath were closed for repair and reopened early May 2013. Unfortunately there was then another minor leak near the newly repaired section, so the canal and towpath were closed again between bridges 212 and 214 from December 2014 to Spring 2015. To find out more about past and present repairs and closures go to: **www.canalrivertrust.org**

The Walk

1. Walk back to the A49, turn left and almost immediately descend through a gate to your left onto the bank of the River Weaver. Turn right and walk under *Acton Swing Bridge* which carries the A49. You walk along the river for about 1½ miles. It is a pleasant walk along the meandering riverside. After a little over ½ mile you can see an attractive black and white trellised bridge ahead which you cross when you reach it. This is over a former loop of the river.

Acton Swing Bridge

2. Continue along the riverside path, past the partially capsized wreck of what was originally a 19th century Norwegian sailing vessel. You will soon come to *Dutton Locks.* These locks were built on a short section of river which was cut to avoid the weir and loop, and so enable boats to navigate this stretch of water.

Partially capsized boat near Dutton Locks

3. Once past *Dutton Locks*, carry on beside the river, noting the huge *Dutton Viaduct* ahead, which carries the railway across the Weaver Valley. Just over 200 yards after passing Dutton Locks, walk over another attractive footbridge, this time a wooden one. Ahead of you is Dutton Farm Park Nature Reserve, which may be worth wandering round if you have the time.

4. When you have crossed over the bridge, turn right through a gate and walk away from the river. You initially walk with the other end of the original course of the waterway to your right. *Dutton Viaduct* continues to dominate the landscape to the left. Carry on away from the main river

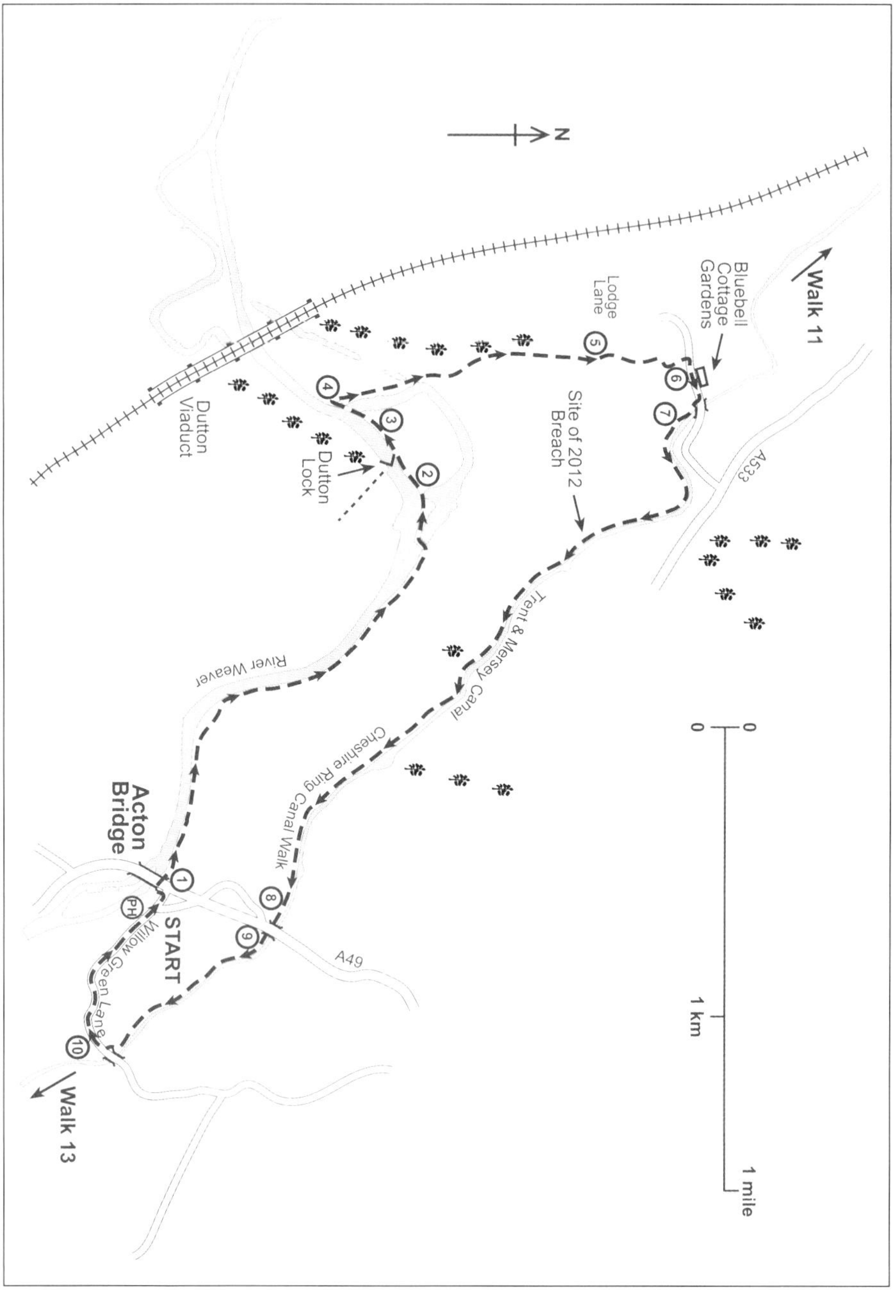
N
Walk 11
Bluebell Cottage Gardens
Lodge Lane
Dutton Viaduct
Dutton Lock
Site of 2012 Breach
A533
River Weaver
Trent & Mersey Canal
Cheshire Ring Canal Walk
Acton Bridge
START
PH
Willow Green Lane
A49
Walk 13
0
1 km
0
1 mile
1
2
3
4
5
6
7
8
9
10

Dutton Viaduct

on a clear wide gravel and earth path. This will take you past a small lake on your left. After passing between trees and bushes on either side, ignore a side gate, but go through one ahead with a Bridleway sign beside it. Continue ahead along a well trodden field path. Go through another gate to join a track where you turn right. Ignore a drive which almost immediately turns sharply right to a farm.

5. The track bears to the left to pass a small wooded area on the right and just before the end of the trees you will see a stile on your right. This is about ⅔ mile after leaving the river. Go over the stile and follow a footpath which soon bends left and takes you along the edge and then through the wood. This woodland is delightful, especially in the spring when it is covered with bluebells. Cross a small bridge over the stream and about 300 yards after entering the wood you come to Lodge Lane. Almost directly ahead is *Bluebell Cottage Gardens.*

6. From the woodland, turn right down Lodge Lane and in under 200 yards you come to the canal. Walk down the slope on your right to reach the towpath.

7. Turn right along the towpath and you will walk with the water to your left for just over two miles to leave the towpath at bridge 207. The canal meanders to the left and then to the right and continues to wind its way slightly above the Weaver valley. About ½ mile after joining the canal you reach the site of the 2012 canal breach which closed the canal and towpath for over 6 months. The repairs have been done to a very high standard. Not only have they noted the central breach line with a plaque but have also provided a seat from where the Weaver Valley (and also the

excellent landscaping) can be admired. The following stretch of water is peaceful and pleasant with grasses, reeds and trees softening the edges of the water and with views of Acton Bridge down to the right.

8. After walking about 1½ miles along the canal you pass some private moorings and just before bridge 209 there are boats belonging to Black Prince Holidays, a cruise hire company. If you wish to visit *Davenport Farm Shop and Tearooms* turn right off the canal at this point and walk for a few yards down the road to reach it. Afterwards return to the towpath.

9. Otherwise, walk under the bridge which carries the A49 and continue along the canal for another half mile until you come to bridge 207. Walk up to your right just before the bridge, to reach Willow Green Lane.

10. Turn right and walk along Willow Green Lane for almost half a mile to return to *The Leigh Arms* and your car.

Acton Swing Bridge

The present Acton Swing Bridge, dates from the early 1930s. It operates electronically and pivots on a pontoon between the main river channel and a minor channel to the south. If you look carefully behind you after passing under the bridge, you can see that there is the arch of an earlier bridge spanning the smaller channel.

Dutton Locks

Dutton Locks, originally constructed in the 1870s, were built to enable the navigation to bypass a weir on the river loop. It is an attractive spot and if you have brought any sustenance, there are a number of picnic tables available. Note the information board and the tiny white lock keeper's cottage. The original river course is now bypassed, and can be seen on the right from the two bridges you pass over.

The Dutton Viaduct

This 60 ft high and 500 yard long viaduct was built in the mid 1830s to carry The Grand Junction Railway over the River Weaver. Joseph Lock was the chief engineer at the time, having taken over from George Stephenson who resigned from the post because he didn't want to work alongside his former assistant.

Places you may wish to stop for refreshment

Bluebell Cottage Gardens and Lodge Lane Nurseries: *01928 713718* **www.bluebellcottage.co.uk** *See Walk 11.*

Davenports Farm shop and Tea Room, Acton Bridge: *01606 853241* **www.davenportsofcheshire.co.uk**

This was a real find. The tea room was awarded The Tea Guild Top Tea award in 2013, and there are a vast number of teas to choose from. The décor is delightful with many allusions to Alice in Wonderland including wall paintings as Charles Dodgson, also known as Lewis Carroll, came from nearby Daresbury. The farm shop is also worth visiting. It is apparently closed Tuesdays and it may be worth looking at their website for opening times before going. At busy times it is advisable to book. Visit it either from the canal or cross the A49 to reach it after your walk.

The Leigh Arms: *01606 853327* **www.leigharms.co.uk**

This large pub serves a good variety of food and drink if you wish to rest here before starting your journey home.

WALK 13

South of Acton Bridge to Anderton

Anderton – Barnton – Little Leigh – Willow Green – The Trent and Mersey Canal – Anderton

Starting point	**The car park by The Anderton Boat Lift. Grid reference: 648753**
Length	**6½ miles**
Allow	**Approximately 2½ hours**
Map	**OS Explorer 267**
By car	**From the A533 north west of Northwich, take the turning to Anderton at the traffic lights immediately north of where the road crosses over The River Weaver. Anderton can also be reached from the A559, following signs and passing thorough Comberbach. Once in the village, follow signs directing you along Uplands Road to the Anderton Boat Lift car park. After turning, cross the canal, turn right and park in the large car park – remembering to use the pay and display which operates for most of the year**

The first part of the walk is relatively uneventful, taking you through *Barnton* and across fields, but the walk back along the canal more than makes up for this. It is a delightful stretch of water, as the canal meanders beneath overhanging trees, and widens in places (the result of former subsidence) to make it even more attractive. To add to the variety, you walk over two of the five tunnels on the Cheshire Ring. Also worthy of note are the flora and fauna. In the spring there are stunning displays of bluebells and lily of the valley on the canal banks, heron can be seen fishing on the water and in the autumn, buzzards circle above the fields.

However, perhaps *The Anderton Boat Lift* is the real 'star' of the walk. It is said to be one of the so called 'Seven wonders of the waterways' and thought by some to be one of the most impressive canal features anywhere in the world or at least in this country. It has been fully restored and is working once more, carrying boats between the Trent and Mersey Canal and the River Weaver.

The Walk

1. Walk down the path to the right of the car park to reach the canal. Turn left then right to cross over the canal on the footbridge which is opposite the *Anderton Boat Lift*. When you are at the other side of the canal, turn left. Walk up Old Road for 200 yards, passing *The Stanley Arms Public House* on your left, to reach New Road. Here you turn left again. Cross the main road where you can and walk for 200 yards passing Bramhalls Park on your right. Immediately after crossing Hough Lane and just before the bridge over the canal, walk down the slope on your right to the canal bank.

2. When you reach the canal, keep right and walk with the water to your left. In under ¼ mile the path ascends away from the canal, and just as you get level with a footbridge below to your left, turn right through a gap at the end of a wall. This leads to Nursery Road. Walk along Nursery Road and in 300 yards you reach Lydyett Lane where you turn left. As you do not pass any pubs or cafés on this walk, you may wish to get sustenance from one of the shops here.

Side view of The Anderton Boat Lift with landscaped surroundings

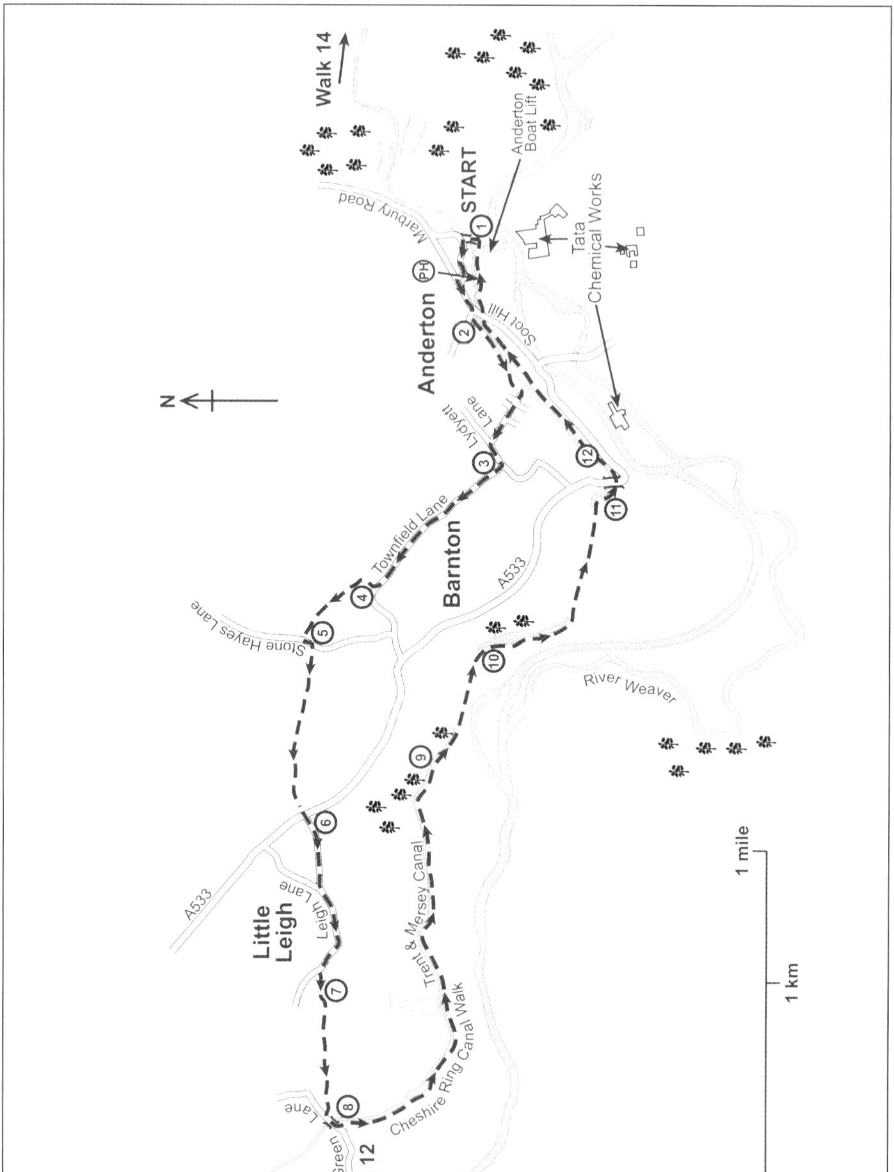

Walk 14
START
Anderton Boat Lift
Marbury Road
PH
Tata Chemical Works
Anderton
Soot Hill
N
Lydyett Lane
Townfield Lane
Barnton
A533
Stone Hayes Lane
River Weaver
Trent & Mersey Canal
A533
Little Leigh
Leigh Lane
Cheshire Ring Canal Walk
Lane
Willow Green
Walk 12
PH
1 mile
1 km
0
0

3. After passing the shops turn right into Townfield Lane. Walk along here for about ½ mile. It is a long straight road but you pass a variety of interesting houses built at different times. Walk past Barnton Library and Rosebank School on your left. A little further along, pass Barnton Community Primary School on your right. Just past here and before the road bends to the left, there is a drive on the right at the far side of the school car park. It is signposted to Barnton Cricket Club. Turn right along the drive.

4. Walk with the school car park to your right, and after about 80 yards turn left off the drive to follow the footpath sign. This footpath takes you through a gate and along the side of a large field with a hedge on your left. Take time to enjoy the views to your right before continuing ahead to reach Stoneheys Lane.

5. Turn left at Stoneheys Lane, then after a few yards, and before you reach some buildings, you will see a footpath sign to the right which you follow. Go through a gate and walk ahead across a large field to a stile at the far side. Once over this stile, cross a small field to go through a gate ahead, then through another small field and through yet another gate into a fourth field. Here you bear left across the corner of the field, to go through another gate which is almost directly under power lines. Follow the footpath sign to the right, walking under the power lines and keeping the hedge to your right until you reach the near right hand corner of the field. Follow the footpath sign through yet another gate, then bear left between two hedges to reach the busy A533 Runcorn Road.

6. Take care crossing this road, and continue ahead down Brakeley Lane. At the T-junction turn left along Church Road into Little Leigh. Pass the church on your right followed by the village hall on your left. The road bears to the right and about 150 yards after the village hall you will see a bridleway which diverges from the road on the left. There is a sign saying it is a Restricted Byway.

7. Bear left down this bridleway and walk along here for just under ½ mile. After a while the bridleway narrows to become a footpath. Continue ahead in the same direction. As you descend towards the canal and River Weaver you will get glorious views towards Acton Bridge ahead. Walk along the left hand side of a woodland before finally descending to join Willow Green Lane. Immediately to your left is a bridge over the canal.

8. Cross the bridge and walk down to your right to join the canal. Turn right and you will walk for just over 3 miles with the water to your left (and at times underneath you!) back to The Anderton Boat Lift. Initially walk through open countryside as the towpath takes you along a ledge above the River Weaver. Note that many parts of the canal along this stretch of water are wider than might be expected. This is the result of local subsidence.

9. The canal meanders through light woodland with over-hanging trees. If you come here in the late spring bluebells and lily of the valley fill the canal banks. To your right you keep getting glimpses of The River Weaver below. Pass bridge 204 and about 1½ miles after joining the canal you come to the 424 yard long *Saltersford Tunnel*. This is the first of two tunnels on this walk, neither of which have a footpath through them. Leave the towpath by walking up past a white house and continue along the clearly defined old horse path following the route of the canal, before descending once more to the towpath. You can see an air vent part way along on your left.

10. Once you are back by the canal, the towpath takes you along a very pleasant stretch of wider water for about ⅓ mile, before you leave it again to walk above the 572 yard long *Barnton Tunnel*. At the entrance to the tunnel, walk up from the canal on a metalled path. Continue along the route of the canal, ignoring a footpath to the left. After a short while you come to a minor road which you cross, and continue ahead in the same direction, passing through some green gates onto a footpath. Ignore a footpath sign you soon see on the right.

Bridge 204

The entrance to Saltersford Tunnel

11. As you descend, make sure you turn right to return to the towpath just before walking over

where the canal emerges on the right. It is easy to miss this and walk straight ahead by mistake. You now walk once more with the water on your left. You will notice that the canal is wider for a short stretch until it turns sharply to the left and passes under the busy A533. To your right, between here and Anderton is the huge *Tata Chemicals* complex at Winnington.

12. After the A533 bridge, walk through a pleasant (although quite noisy) wooded area for around ⅔ mile before reaching bridge 200. Once under this bridge, continue along the towpath and in about ¼ mile you return to *The Anderton Boat Lift* followed by the path back to the car park and your car.

    If you are able, it is recommended you stop to look at The Anderton Boat Lift and perhaps go in the visitors centre. If you have time you may even wish to take a trip on the lift down to the River Weaver.

The Anderton Boat Lift

01606 786777 **www.andertonboatlift.co.uk**

The lift was designed by Edwin Clark and built in 1875 by Leader Williams in order to connect the Trent and Mersey Canal with the busy Weaver Navigation which was 50 ft below. It consisted of two huge water filled tanks each of which could hold two narrow boats. It was originally run on steam, but after major repairs in 1908, the steam was replaced by electricity. The lift closed in 1983, but after gaining Heritage Lottery Funding, was reopened in 2002 after two years of work costing £7 million. The lift is now in full working order, using the original 1875 hydraulic design. It attracts visitors in its own right, in addition to opening up the connection between the two waterways again.

The Anderton Boat Lift from above with Tata Chemical Works, Winnington, behind

Barnton

It is said that Barnton holds the record of being the largest village in England. It was mentioned in the Domesday Book, covers 750 acres and stands 100 feet above The Weaver valley. By the mid 18th century the village had a stable

population of about 200. The development of the local salt industry resulted in the need to improve transportation and The Weaver Navigation Act in 1721, followed by the construction of The Trent and Mersey Canal a few years later, resulted in an influx of labourers and craftsmen to the area. Between 1775 and 1815 the population of Barnton doubled and between 1815 and 1845 it doubled again.

The Saltersford and Barnton Tunnels

These two tunnels, amongst the earliest to be built on the canal network, were constructed by the 'cut and cover' method. Neither are straight and their narrow width meant wide beam boats could not travel from Preston Brook to Middlewich, which had been hoped for initially. Boats are also unable to pass each other in the tunnels – note the strict times for travelling each way which are set out at either end.

For more information about tunnels with no towpaths see 'Preston Brook Tunnel' in walk 11.

Tata Chemicals, formerly Brunner Mond

In 1874 John Brunner and Ludwig Mond founded Brunner Mond Chemical Works in Winnington. This is now a huge complex. Other works were also built in the area (see walks 15, 18 and 21).This part of Cheshire was an ideal location, as the local salt was used as the main raw material to manufacture soda ash. For the disposal of the soda ash waste they used land which had subsided as the result of salt extraction underneath and could not therefore be built on. Such action produced dangerous alkaline lime beds which unfortunately contaminated the land for many years. In recent years there has been much reclamation of this land (see walks 14 and 15). In 2006, Brunner Mond was bought by Tata Chemicals.

Places you may wish to stop for refreshment

The Stanley Arms: *01606 77661* **www.stanleyarmsanderton.co.uk**
Not tried by the author but was apparently refurbished in 2012.
The Anderton Boat Lift Visitors Centre, café and shop: *01606 786777* **www.andertonboatlift.co.uk**
There is an excellent café at the visitors centre with a wonderful view down onto the boat lift. There is also an interesting shop and you can book a trip down on the boat lift. There are attractive well- landscaped grounds below the visitors centre. Note the centre is closed over the winter, as is the boat lift.

WALK 14
Anderton to Marston

Anderton – The Bridgewater Canal – Marston – Neumann's Flashes – Anderton Nature Park - The River Weaver – Anderton

Starting point	**The car park by The Anderton Boat Lift. Grid reference: 648753**
Length	**4½ miles**
Allow	**1½-2 hours**
Map	**OS Explorer 267**
By car	**From the A533 north west of Northwich, take the turning to Anderton at the traffic lights immediately north of where the road crosses over The River Weaver. Anderton can also be reached from the A559, following signs and passing thorough Comberbach. Once in the village, follow signs directing you along Uplands Road to the Anderton Boat Lift Car Park. After turning, cross the canal, turn right and park in the large car park – remembering to use the pay and display which operates for most of the year**

This is perhaps one of the pleasantest and most interesting walks on the Cheshire Ring. Although it is short, it passes many places of interest and there are few roads to walk along. The star of this walk is the *Anderton Boat Lift* which has been fully restored and is working once more, carrying boats between the Trent and Mersey Canal and the River Weaver. For more details see Walk 13. *The Lion Salt Works* at Marston is also worthy of note - as it was the last in Britain to produce salt by the traditional method of evaporating brine in open pans. Between these two is a very pleasant stretch of canal. The walk back is no less pleasing, taking you past *Neumann's Flashes,* through the reclaimed land of *Anderton Nature Park* and along the banks of Witton Brook and the River Weaver. It is difficult to believe that a century ago this area was surrounded by salt mines and industrial waste.

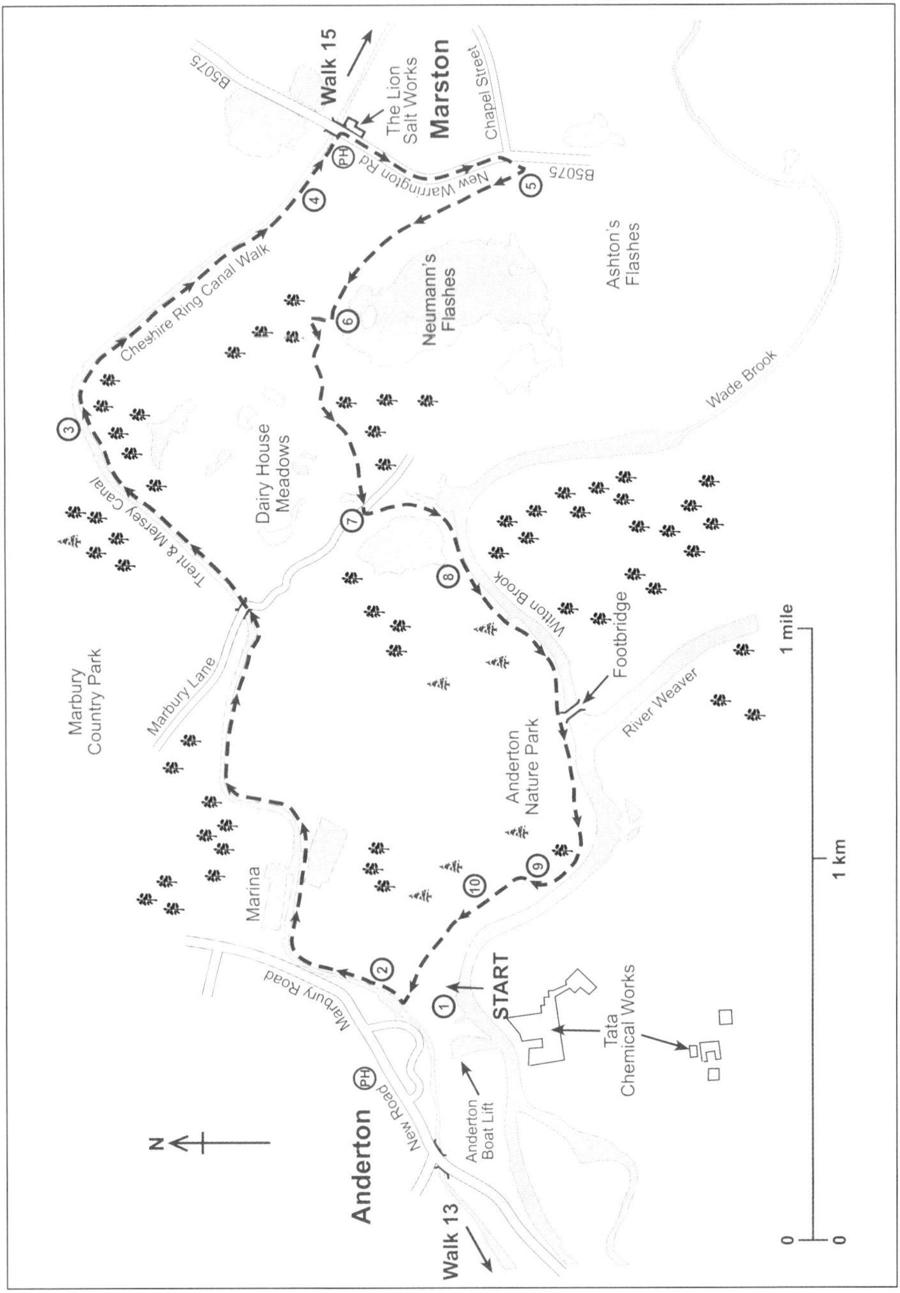

Walk 15
The Lion Salt Works
Marston
Chapel Street
B5075
PH
New Warrington Rd
B5075
Cheshire Ring Canal Walk
Neumann's Flashes
Ashton's Flashes
Wade Brook
Dairy House Meadows
Trent & Mersey Canal
Marbury Country Park
Marbury Lane
Witton Brook
Footbridge
River Weaver
Anderton Nature Park
Marina
START
Tata Chemical Works
Marbury Road
PH
Anderton Boat Lift
New Road
Anderton
N
Walk 13
1
2
3
4
5
6
7
8
9
10
0
1 mile
0
1 km

The Walk

1. Walk down the path that leads from the car park to the canal, with the *Anderton Boat Lift* to your left. Once on the towpath, turn right, and you will walk for two miles with the water on your left, until you leave the canal at bridge 193. The whole of this stretch is extremely attractive, as the canal meanders through pleasant woodland and open countryside.

2. Walk away from the boat lift passing gardens backing onto the canal. After walking under a bridge the canal bears to the right and you come to Anderton Marina. This marina is of a considerable size. Walk up and over a channel leading to another part of the marina, then return to the canal side. The canal bends to the left and right as it enters a pleasant wooded section - to the right is *Anderton Nature Park* and to the left, over the canal is *Marbury Country Park*. They are connected by a black and white trellised footbridge.

3. Just before the canal bends sharply to the right, you pass the site of a huge canal breach which occurred in 1907. The breach was caused by

The Trent and Mersey Canal near Anderton

subsidence due to the collapse of underground workings belonging to the local Marston Hall Mine. This mine, one of the many *Salt Workings in the Marston area,* was located to the left of the bend. The half mile of canal after the bend was only cut in 1958. This replaced the original route which was about to collapse as the result of more underground salt workings.

Entrance to Anderton Marina

The Salt Barge Pub, Marston

4. Soon after the end of the straight stretch of canal, pass a path on the right which leads to The *Salt Barge Public House.* Continue for a few more yards, then turn right to leave the towpath just before bridge 193, walking beside the site of the former salt store for *The Lion Salt Works.* Turn right at the road. Walk through *Marston,* passing the entrance to *The Lion Salt Works* on your left and *The Salt Barge Pub* on your right. Continue along the road and out of the village.

5. About ⅓ mile after leaving the canal and just past Chapel Street on your left, you will see some gates on the right leading to *Neumann's Flashes and Ashton Flashes.* Turn right here, go through the gates then keep far right to walk on a wide well made path with fences to either side, initially almost going back in the direction you have come from. Do not go on the other well made path which is ahead of you. You will soon see *Neuman's Flashes* on your left. From here, all the way back to your car, you will be walking through *Northwich Community Woodlands.* Note the pipes on your right, and at various points along the rest of the walk. These are associated with old industrial salt workings. Pass a bird hide on your left and continue along the path.

6. Slightly under ½ mile after joining the path you reach a gate ahead and a path to your right signposted to *Dairy House Meadow*. Go right to follow the sign and very soon bend sharply to the left. Note there are more pipes along here. Continue along this path and about 250 yards after the bend, the path diverges. Keeping the bench on your right, bear left here, following a sign to Marbury Lane which you will reach almost 350 yards further on.

7. Go through the gate, turn left along Marbury Lane, and after about 50 yards turn right into *Anderton Nature Park*. Walk into the nature park and in under 50 yards you come to a T-junction. There is an information board here about Sand Martins. Turn left at this junction, and the path will soon lead you down to the banks of Witton Brook which is a tributary of The River Weaver. However, the reed beds to your left restrict the view of the water in the summer.

8. Continue along the path beside Witton Brook for about ⅓ mile until you come to a trellised footbridge, after which the tributary joins the main river. Do not cross the footbridge but continue ahead down some shallow steps to walk along the banks of what is now The River Weaver. The River Weaver soon bears to the right. Note more pipes related to the former salt industry in the area.

9. Go over two wooden 'bridges' and almost immediately after the second one you come to a T-junction. This is about ⅓ mile after the footbridge. There is a path to your right, a field gate ahead to your right and a main path to your left which carries on along the river. However, you want the path which cuts through a grassy area ahead and slightly left, and leads away from the river. If in doubt, there is a sign that directs you to the *Boat Lift*. (If you do not wish to walk across the grass, keep left along the river for a little longer until the main path bears away from the river.)

10. At the end of the grassy area, bear right along the main wide path which takes you up through a lightly wooded area. Continue ahead along the path, through an interesting 'gate' made up of two metal butteflies, and return to the car park and your car.

The Anderton Boat Lift

See Walk 13.

Anderton Nature Park and Dairy House Meadow

This nature park and the meadows are on reclaimed wasteland, and like the area around the flashes they are especially interesting, in that, due to the saltiness of the soil, many plants, usually seen in coastal environments, can be found here.

Marbury Country Park

Marbury Hall, which once overlooked Budworth Mere was demolished in 1968, but its grounds, including restored gardens are now open to the public as Marbury Country Park.

Salt workings in the Marston area

You might not believe it today but Marston was once surrounded by salt workings and salt mines. Just before the bend and the straightened 1958 section of canal, there was Marston Hall Mine. Marston Old Mine and Adelaide Mine were on the left of the canal between the bend and the village - the latter being on land now occupied by a flash, just north of bridge 193. In Marston itself, apart from The Lion Salt Works, there were Crystal Mine and New Zealand Mine behind The Salt Barge Public House and Nelson Mine and Blackburne's Mine just to the south of the village. It is not surprising therefore that Marston has suffered from the proximity of these salt workings and subsidence in the past has caused the collapse and demolition of a number of houses. Note the spaces throughout the village where buildings once stood.

The Lion Salt Works

www.lionsaltworks.org

This open pan salt works was opened in 1842 by The Thompson Family and produced fishery, bay, crystal and lump salt. After the brine was pumped from the ground and evaporated, the blocks of crystals were taken by the work's fleet of narrow boats from Marston to Anderton. Here, they were lowered on the Anderton Boat Lift and taken in larger vessels via the Weaver and Mersey to Liverpool. From here the salt was finally exported to amongst other places, India and Canada. The works struggled through as the last place producing salt by the 'open pan' method but eventually closed in 1986. After being derelict for a number of years, it was reopened as a working museum in 2015, with money from the Lottery Heritage Fund. A visit can be highly recommended.

Northwich Community Woodlands

In recent years a strategic Programme of Reclamation has taken place here to transform the derelict land, much of it contaminated lime beds, into a nature park. The 323 hectare community woodland is made up of: Ashton's Flashes, Neunann's Flashes, Dairy House Meadows, Anderton Nature Park, Witton Flash and Witton Hill Meadows.

Neumann's Flashes and Ashton's Flashes

Flashes are lakes formed by subsidence as the result of former salt workings. These two are the largest in the Northwich area. Neumann's Flashes was caused by a salt mine collapsing in 1873 and Ashton's Flashes was the result of approximately 6,000,000 tons of water flowing into mine workings after subsidence in 1880. In the 1950s both flashes were filled with lime waste from the local chemical industry. The lime beds remained derelict for years. Both flashes are now part of The Northwich Community Woodland. Neumann's Flashes is of particular interest as it is a permanent lake which attracts many breeding and migrating birds. The saltiness in the soil has meant that certain plants you would not expect, such as several types of orchids, have become established in the area.

Places you may wish to stop for refreshment

The Stanley Arms, Anderton: *01606 77661* **www.stanleyarmsanderton.co.uk**
See walk 13.
The Salt Barge, Marston*: 01606 212525. An old mining community pub with plenty of character.*
The Anderton Boat Lift Café: *01606 786777* **www.andertonboatlift.co.uk**
See walk 13.

WALK 15
Marston to Rudheath

Marston – The Trent and Mersey Canal – Rudheath - Griffiths Park – East Northwich – Ashton's Flashes – Marston

Starting point	**Marston, north of Northwich. Grid reference: 670754**
Length	**4½ miles**
Allow	**1½-2 hours**
Map	**OS Explorer 267**
By car	**Marston is on the B 5075 between Northwich and the A559. To reach it, either drive north from the centre of Northwich, or south from the A559 at Higher Marston. Park on the B5075 in Marston. But if this is difficult, park in the large layby just south of the B5391 junction. Walk back through Marston to the canal**

This is a varied and slightly different walk. The walk circles the north east side of *Northwich,* and as a consequence includes a stretch of road. You also pass a large industrial complex by the canal, although this in its own way is interesting. There is much variety in this walk including *Northwich Community Woodlands,* the salt flats and the village of Marston with of course the *Lion Salt Works.* As the roads round here can be busy, you may wish to do this walk outside working hours.

The Walk

1. Walk through Marston towards the canal with the Salt Barge pub to your left and *Lion Salt Works* to your right. Just before the bridge walk down the path to your left to join the canal. *The Lion Salt Works* salt store used to be located here by the canal bridge. You may wish to read the two information boards about the salt works, one is by its main entrance and the other is near the canal.

2. Once on the towpath, turn right to walk with the water on your left for almost two miles before leaving just before bridge 185 in Rudheath. Walk under the bridge in Marston. Immediately to you your right is the *Lion Salt Works*. Pass Wincham Industrial Estate on the far side of the canal, behind which are Northwich Victoria Football Club's stadium and grounds. After a mile the canal turns sharply to the right at Wincham Bend and on the inside of the bend there is a dwelling with a large garden.

3. Soon after the bend, the landscape changes dramatically. After walking under bridge 189 you pass The Lamb Inn, Olympus Narrowboats and some boats moored along the canal, followed by a large industrial complex which spans the canal. This appears to be in a continuous state of evolution, and is part of the huge *Tata Chemicals Company*. Pass under a number of pipes, then up and over a derelict arm of the canal. At this point look to the left where you can see green fields, which, although they may be on reclaimed land, are a contrast to the immediate area. Ignore two footpaths which lead off the canal, and continue along the towpath which runs between the factories on either side.

Tata Chemical Works

4. When you have passed under a high wooden bridge, you come to the end of the main works complex. Go under another bridge then past part derelict, part restored, land to your right. Just before bridge 185, cut through the grassy area on your right which leads you to a path. Keep left along the path which runs a little way from, but almost parallel to the canal, to reach some metal posts. Walk through the posts onto the end of Farm Road. If for any reason you missed the turn off, when you come to bridge 185, cut straight across to your right and you should come to the posts and the end of Farm Road.

5. Once past the posts do not walk down Farm Road but turn immediately right. Go past a metal gateway and onto a sandy coloured path which leads you between bushes into Griffiths Park. After about 100 yards the path bends to the left. Here you have a choice. You may either stay on the

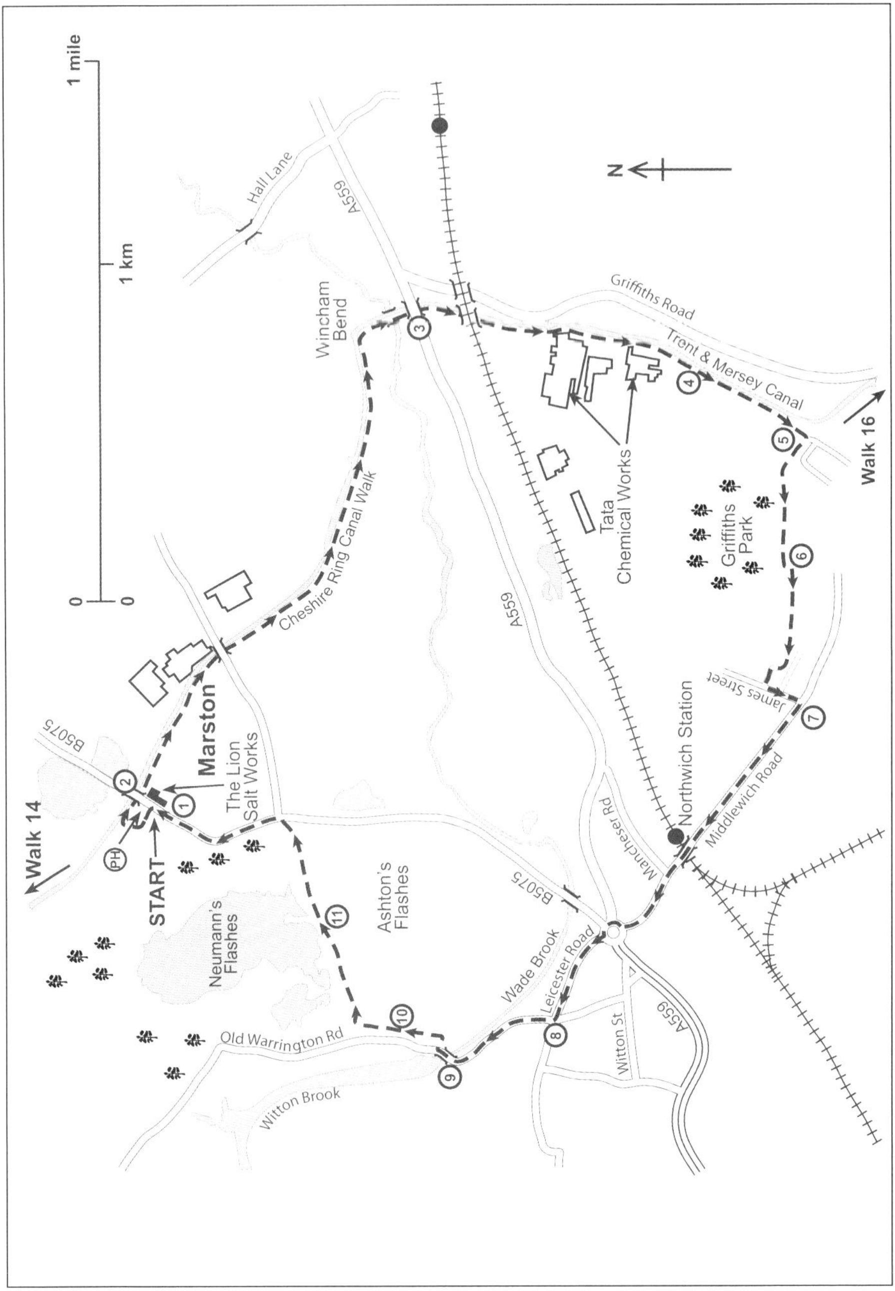

1 mile
1 km
0
0
N
Hall Lane
A559
Wincham Bend
Griffiths Road
Trent & Mersey Canal
Walk 16
Tata Chemical Works
Griffiths Park
James Street
Northwich Station
Middlewich Road
Manchester Rd
A559
Cheshire Ring Canal Walk
B5075
Marston
The Lion Salt Works
Walk 14
PH
START
Neumann's Flashes
Ashton's Flashes
B5075
Wade Brook
Leicester Road
Witton St
A559
Old Warrington Rd
Witton Brook

path which bears gently to the right and then continues along the right hand edge of a playing field to reach its far side in just over 200 yards. Alternatively, climb up the path which rises to your right, and continue up until you reach a bench. Here, if you walk for a few yards to your right you will see an interesting metal insect sculpture. Retrace your steps back to the lower path and turn right. You will continue along the right hand edge of the playing field towards the buildings in front of you.

Insect sculpture above Griffiths Park

6. At the far side of the playing field, do not bear left on the main path along the back of the field but instead bear slightly right to continue ahead largely in the same direction along another path. This takes you firstly alongside a high fence on your left with derelict spaces behind, and eventually to terraced housing. Continue along the path, and about ¼ mile after leaving the park you keep to the right to join Liverpool Street. At the end of Liverpool Street is a T-junction. Turn left here into James Street at the end of which is the B5082.

7. Turn right, and walk along the B5082 for about ½ mile. Unfortunately there is no avoiding this stretch of road. Go over the railway line and past Northwich Station, then straight ahead across the traffic lights, continuing on this road until you come to a roundabout. Here you will go ahead down Leicester Street. To reach it, go round the right side of the roundabout, crossing two roads including The New Warrington Road which, although it is signposted towards Warrington, Marston and the Lion Salt Works, you do not take. Leicester Street has a 40mph sign and at present there is a Pure Gym to its left.

8. After walking about 300 yards along Leicester Street you will see a 'No through Road' sign to your right also indicated to lead to a Household Waste Tip and Recycling Centre. Turn right here along Old Warrington Road. After about 150 yards, walk under a decorated pipe and past a road on your left which leads to the household waste site then pass through

an open metal gate and past a 20mph sign. You are now in part of *Northwich Community Woodlands.*

9. You soon bear right to cross Witton Brook at Witton Bridge. Almost immediately after the bridge, turn right and climb up to the edge of *Ashton's Flashes.* Once you are up, turn left along the path.

10. Walk with the flash to your right for about 300 yards before reaching a wooden gate. Pass through here and turn right to walk along a pleasant tree lined path between *Ashton's Flashes* on your right and *Neumann's Flashes* on your left. If in doubt, there is a wooden signpost which directs you towards Marston. If you have time, half way along this path turn left and walk to the bird hide which gives you a wonderful view across the water-filled *Neumann's Flashes.* Walk 14 takes you along the far side of this flash.

11. Continue along the path. In about ¼ mile pass through a gate and you will see New Warrington Road ahead to your right. Go through another gate

View of Neumann's Flashes from a bird hide

to reach the road and turn left. Walk along here with care and in about ¼ mile you will return to Marston and your car.

Salt workings in the Marston area

See Walk 14.

The Lion Salt Works

www.lionsaltworks.westcheshiremuseums.co.uk *See Walk 14.*

Tata Chemicals, formerly Brunner Mond

See walk 13.

Northwich

Northwich grew at the confluence of the River Dane and River Weaver, hence its Roman name of Condate meaning confluence. Over the centuries the area has been exploited for its salt, resulting in a huge amount of subsidence in and around Northwich. It is only in recent years that serious stabilisation has been undertaken, and now that this has taken place there are plans for extensive urban regeneration. The Tata Chemical Company Works at Winnington dominates much of the north of the town. For more information on the Salt Industry in Cheshire, see the introduction.

Northwich Community Woodlands

See walk 14.

Neumann's Flashes and Ashton's Flashes

See Walk 14.

Places you may wish to stop for refreshment

The Salt Barge Pub, Marston*: 01606 212525. See walk 14.*

WALK 16
Rudheath to Whatcroft

Rudheath – The Trent and Mersey Canal – Whatcroft – Higher Shurlach – East Northwich – The Trent and Mersey Canal – Rudheath

Starting point	**By The Old Broken Cross Pub on the B5082, Rudheath. Grid reference: 683732**
Length	**5-5½ miles**
Allow	**Approximately 2 hours**
Map	**OS Explorer 267**
By car	**Park by The Old Broken Cross Pub by the canal bridge on the B5082 south east of Northwich. If full, park at the end of Field Road (3rd on the right, towards Northwich), and start and end the walk at Direction 10**

This walk is one of contrasts, as you walk through both the outskirts of Northwich and also some delightful countryside. It should be noted that unfortunately it seems the HS2 rail line will cross the canal twice on this walk, so after the mid 2020s it is worth checking for possible towpath closures. See Direction 2 for an alternative route.

The Walk

1. Walk through the car park and onto the towpath. Turn right. You will walk with the water to your left for just over 2 miles to leave the canal at bridge 179. Continue along the towpath behind some modern houses. Pass under bridge 183 then under the A556 on bridge 182A. A large distribution centre can be seen to your left. Walk past 'Park Farm Marina' on your right then you soon come to Bridge 181.

2. Hopefully you can continue along the towpath from here. However, from the mid 2020s onwards it may be temporarily closed in order to build two HS2 rail bridges over the canal between here and where you leave at

bridge 179. If so, leave at bridge 181, turn right and walk along the road for ½ mile until you reach some cross roads. *Riverside Organics* is to your left. Turn right here up Shurlach Lane to re-join the walk at Direction 5. The shortened walk is now just under 5 miles long.

3. Otherwise continue ahead along the towpath. After bridge 181 pass Oakwood Marina on your left. Walk past a large 'wide' also on the left, after which the canal bends to the right. Continue under a railway bridge and along this delightful and quiet stretch of water, though this may change in the future if HS2 is built across the canal here.

4. Leave the canal to your right just before bridge 179 and turn right. Walk along the narrow Manor Lane. Pass Old Lane on your right in just under ¼ mile, then dip down and up again before passing the other end of Old Lane. Approximately ⅔ mile after leaving the canal, you come to a cross roads with a small green in the middle. Just before here to your left you will see *Riverside Organics.* This is a lovely café and farm shop, which can easily be returned to by car at the end of the walk if you do not wish to stop at this point.

Remains of a wreck in a 'wide'

The second 'wide'

Bridge 179

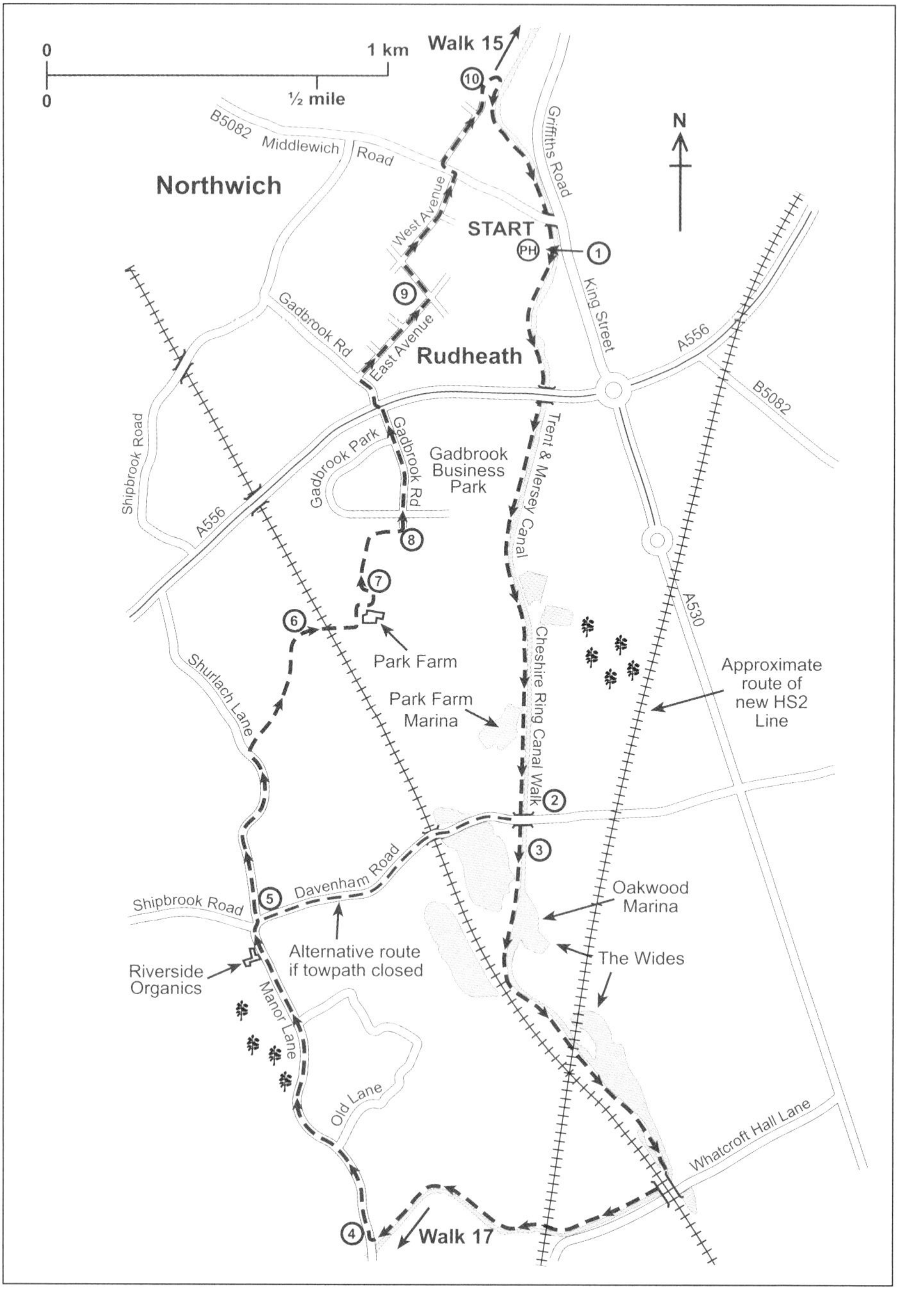
0
1 km
0
½ mile
Walk 15
10
B5082 Middlewich Road
Griffiths Road
N
Northwich
West Avenue
START
PH
1
9
Gadbrook Rd
East Avenue
Rudheath
King Street
A556
B5082
Shipbrook Road
Gadbrook Park
Gadbrook Rd
Gadbrook Business Park
Trent & Mersey Canal
A556
8
7
6
Park Farm
A530
Shurlach Lane
Cheshire Ring Canal Walk
Approximate route of new HS2 Line
Park Farm Marina
2
3
Davenham Road
5
Shipbrook Road
Oakwood Marina
The Wides
Alternative route if towpath closed
Riverside Organics
Manor Lane
Old Lane
Whatcroft Hall Lane
4
Walk 17

5. At the cross roads continue ahead up Shurlach Lane. Do not go down the road to the left nor the one to the right. Shurlach Lane bears slightly right then left and about ⅓ mile after the crossroads you reach a metal gate on your right. This is soon after a footpath and telegraph pole on your left. Opposite the gate is a small footpath sign. Turn right here to follow the sign and although the gate is chained there is a gap in the hedge to the left of it which you go through. Once thorough the gap, walk ahead along the side of the field, keeping the hedge on your right. At the end of the field you reach a driveway.

6. Turn right to walk along the driveway which takes you over a railway line. Once over the railway line, turn left to go over a stile. This takes you to a gravelled path which turns right then left, after which it becomes a less clear field path. However, it is still possible to follow it as it meanders down towards a small stream and business park ahead. In high summer the field can be full of nettles, so it may be advisable to wear long trousers!

7. Cross the stream on the footbridge, then follow the path as it leads up, climbing to the left of the business park which is ahead of you. Continue ahead with a car park to the left and buildings to the right. The path turns right into School Road. Walk along School Road to reach Gadbrook Road.

8. Turn left into Gadbrook Road which takes you through the well landscaped Gadbrook Park Business Park. Walk straight ahead for about ¼ mile until you come to the A556. Descend to the underpass on the right to walk below the main road and once through the underpass continue ahead and take the first right down East Avenue. Walk along here for just under ¼ mile, passing Grange Road and South Drive on the left then take the third left along Central Road. You will notice that there are a number of well maintained and attractive gardens in this older, well established council estate.

9. Once on Central Road, pass Central Grove on your left, then when you reach West Avenue, turn right. Walk along West Avenue for just under ¼ mile, passing North Drive on the right, to reach the B5082, Middlewich Road. Turn left, cross the main road with care, and after a few yards you come to Farm Road on the right, which you will turn down. Walk along Farm Road and soon after passing St John's Close on your left you come to the end of the road.

10. Go ahead between green posts and onto a footpath. Once you are through the posts, turn right through a gap in the undergrowth (or across what is simply grass in the winter) to reach The Trent and Mersey Canal. If you have been on walk 15 you will recognise this. Turn right onto the towpath to walk with the water on your left for about ¼ mile. After passing under Bridge 184, where the B5082 crosses the canal, turn right at The Old Broken Cross Pub to return to your car.

Submerged boats in the 'wides'

Wides are lakes connected to the canal as the result of former salt mining subsidence. From the 1870s onwards, The Bridgewater Canal Company bought a number of steam tugs knows as 'Little Packets', and by 1881 there were 26 of these operating on The Bridgwater and other nearby canals including the Trent and Mersey Canal. They were in regular use until the 1920s after which time some were scrapped and some were converted to diesel. The last of the diesel powered boats were brought here and sunk in the 1950s, in a controversial move by British Waterways to reduce their fleet of boats. In recent years most have been raised and restored. See Walk 4 for more information on packet boats.

Places you may wish to stop for refreshment

The Old Broken Cross Pub, Rudheath: *01606 333111*

Riverside Organics: *01606 46258*

This farm café offers drinks, food and delicious home made ice creams, and there is an organic food shop selling organic meat and other foodstuffs produced on the farm and locally. Not only does it make a welcome stop, it is also well worth supporting.

If you wish to return here after the walk, return to the A530/A556 junction, continue ahead down the A530 and after about 1 mile turn right at the cross roads. Continue along here to the cross roads you passed on the walk, and you will see Riverside Organics ahead on your left.

The Cheshire Grill, Lach Dennis: *01606 41100* **www.grill.co.uk/cheshire**

Although not immediately next to the canal, this pub can be recommended for both food and drink. To reach Lach Dennis return to the A530/A556 junction, continue ahead down the A530 and after a mile turn left at the cross roads. Bear right in the village and you will see the pub on your right.

WALK 17

Whatcroft to The Big Lock, Middlewich

The Big Lock, Middlewich – Yatehouse Green – Drakelow Lane – Whatcroft – The Trent and Mersey Canal – The Big Lock, Middlewich

Starting point	**The Big Lock, Middlewich. Grid reference: 702668**
Length	**8½ miles. Due to some busy stretches of road, this walk is not suitable for children**
Allow	**3-3½ hours**
Map	**OS Explorer 267**
By car	**If coming along the A54 from the east and the M6 Junction 18, go over the canal in the centre of Middlewich, pass the junction with the A533 Sandbach Road then take a right hand filter onto Pepper Street. This is just under 250 yards after the junction and leads you to a short stretch of road with grass either side of it. If coming into Middlewich from the west, you turn left 250 yards before the A533 junction. Once on Pepper Street, turn immediately to the left. Webb's Lane bends to the right and you continue up the road until you see the Big Lock Public House on your right just before a sharp left hand bend. Park near the pub, or in its car park if you intend to stop there on your return**

This is the longest circular walk along the Cheshire Ring. The first half from Middlewich up to Whatcroft is along some little used footpaths (mainly, but not always, well signposted) and some stretches of road. The return section is along a delightful section of the canal which is as pleasant as any you will encounter on the whole of The Ring. It is quite a long section of easy towpath walking, and along much of the way you can see the River Dane meandering down to your right. It is suggested you wear long trousers to avoid nettles and other skin irritants on the little used sections of the footpaths.

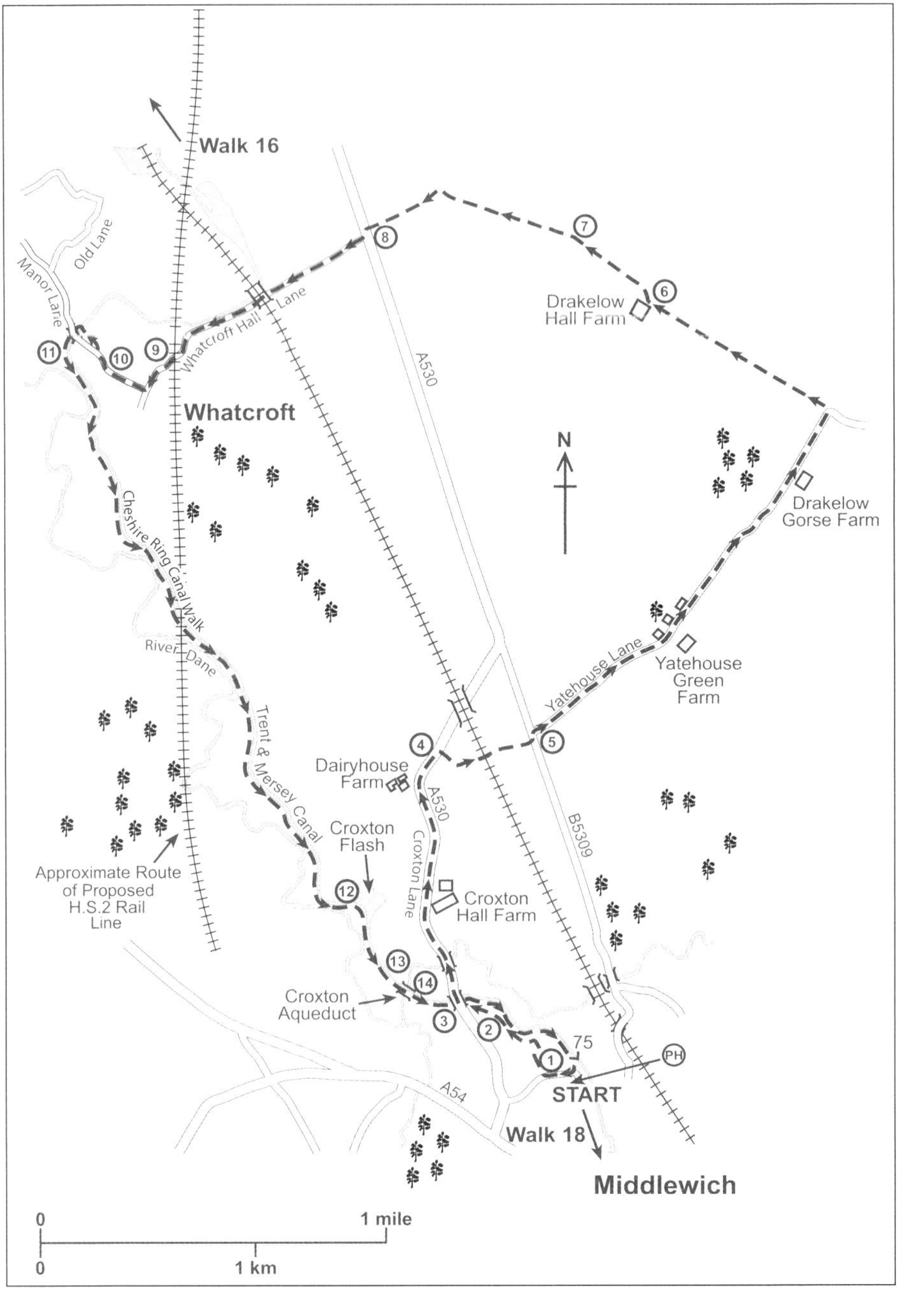
Walk 16
Old Lane
Manor Lane
Whatcroft Hall Lane
A530
Drakelow Hall Farm
Whatcroft
N
Drakelow Gorse Farm
Cheshire Ring Canal Walk
River Dane
Trent & Mersey Canal
Yatehouse Lane
Yatehouse Green Farm
Dairyhouse Farm
A530
Croxton Lane
B5309
Croxton Flash
Croxton Hall Farm
Approximate Route of Proposed H.S.2 Rail Line
Croxton Aqueduct
75
PH
START
A54
Walk 18
Middlewich
0
1 mile
0
1 km

The proposed route of the new HS2 rail line is set to pass across two points of the walk: a little way before you turn right off Whatcroft Hall Lane, and also part way along the canal. This may cause diversions or even completely close footpaths for a while during its construction, and is bound to have some impact on the peace of the area.

The Walk

1. Walk away from the centre of Middlewich, continuing along Webb's Lane which bends sharply to the left at The Big Lock Public House. 150 yards after the bend, the road veers to the left, and there is a footpath sign on the right which you take. This track passes between fences and after about 125 yards bends round right and left, before going between houses to join The Windings (ignore any tracks which lead to the right). Walk down The Windings and just after house no. 6 on your right you will see a footpath, which you take to the canal side. Be careful not to miss this.

2. Turn left at the canal and almost immediately, at the end of the wooden fence, turn left again to follow a footpath sign away from the canal. This takes you up alongside a fence on your left hand side to reach a metal gate. Go along a path, through another gate, then walk across a field and through a third gate to reach at the A530 Croxton Lane.

3. Turn right at Croxton Lane to walk over the canal. Continue along Croxton Lane for approximately ¾ mile. For much of the way you can walk on the grass verge, but take care, especially when going over the River Dane Bridge. Pass Croxton Hall Farm on your right and Dairy House Farm on your left, at which point the road bends to the right.

4. Just before the next field boundary on your left there is a footpath on your right which you take. At the time of writing the field was full of healthy wheat with no discernable footpath, although it is a right of way. The route of the footpath leads you at right angles away from the road and turns left when you are in line with a large oak tree ahead to your left. However if there are crops in the field, it might be advisable to turn left sooner and when you reach the left hand side of the field turn right and walk with the hedge and railway line to your left until you reach the oak tree. Near the oak tree you will see another footpath sign which leads to your left to cross a stile and takes you over the railway track. Take great

care and look both ways! The whole of this section appears to be walked infrequently, and is overgrown in places but at least there are signs to follow. Once you are over the track, walk across the field at right angles to the railway line, to reach *King Street.*

5. Cross over *King Street*, turn left then almost immediately right down Yatehouse Lane. You will walk along Yatehouse Lane for about 1¼ miles until you come to where the road bends sharply to the right and Drakelow Lane joins from the left. Turn left down here, keeping a yellow grit container to your right. Do not be tempted to take any of the earlier tracks to the left as Drakelow Lane is obvious when you reach it. It is a right of way, even though it may look like a private road, but as works traffic associated with a gas works uses it, take care if you are here during the week.

6. After walking along Drakelow Lane for just over ½ mile you come to Drakelow Hall Farm on your left, and here you continue ahead in the same direction through the farmyard. Go through a gate which usually appears to be open, then look carefully for a footpath sign on your right taking you through an exercise paddock. On leaving the paddock, turn left, and walk with the hedge on your left, apart from where you have to deviate round a rough boggy patch. It can be wet in this field so choose carefully where you walk. At the far left corner of the field there is a gate by a 'Restricted Byway' sign.

7. Go through the gate onto the Restricted Byway. Walk ahead along a wide grassy track. After a while, where the track bears right to join one of the roads in the gas complex, don't follow it, but continue on a narrower path ahead. Cross another track leading to a the gas complex then soon cross over a road which leads from the complex to the main road. Continue ahead in the same direction for a few more yards, then turn left down a wide but largely clear path which leads you through a narrow band of trees to reach the main road in about ¼ mile.

8. Cross the busy A530 with care and turn left then almost immediately right to go down Whatcroft Hall Lane. After passing under a railway bridge you can see the canal to your right but as the towpath is the other side, you can't join it yet. It is somewhere near here that the new HS2 rail line will be crossing the route.

9. Continue past some building on your right to reach a wooden fence, also on your right. Ignore a footpath sign over a blocked stile in the fence and continue along the road. You soon reach a driveway which is at the end of the fencing. This is about ¾ mile after joining Whatcroft Hall Lane. Turn right down the driveway.

10. Ignore a padlocked gate on your right, and continue along the driveway. Where another drive joins from the left, turn right to go down a clear enclosed permissive path. In a short time this bears to the right and in just under 300 yards leads you through a metal gate to reach a bridge over the canal. Cross the bridge and go down on the right to reach the towpath.

11. Turn right onto the towpath, to walk for just under 3 miles along what at present is a very pleasant stretch of canal. Soon after bridge 179 you will see The River Dane to your right. Pass the parkland of Bostock Hall, a school for children with learning difficulties, behind trees to your left. In the woods at the far side of the canal between Bridge 177 and 176 it is said that there are the remains of old wagon tippers, a remnant from the days when there were clay pits in the area. Note also the flat topped bridges, built so they could be raised if subsidence occurred.

Peaceful stretch of the Trent and Mersey Canal leading to bridge 179

Note, it is somewhere near bridge 177 that the proposed HS2 rail line will cross the canal on a viaduct spanning the Dane valley and during its construction parts of the towpath may be blocked off. If you are aware that work has begun it may be worth finding out more before starting the walk but it must be pointed out that even if the line is built, it will not happen for a number of years. In the long term, although the towpath will almost certainly be reinstated, the peace of this short section of the walk may well be compromised. Who knows though – the viaduct may become a thing of beauty to be admired in the future!

12. Further on you pass Croxton Flash, a lake connected to the canal, caused by salt mining subsidence. Throughout most of this stretch of canal, you

will notice The River Dane which meanders below to your right and almost touches the canal a number of times until the canal passes over it on *The Croxton Aqueduct.*

13. At the *Croxton Aqueduct* the canal passes over The River Dane. Almost immediately after this you will see an information plaque. On it are some interesting facts about the aqueduct and surrounding area and also a guided walk around Middlewich.

    At this point you may wish to deviate from the route and follow a short (approximately 15 minutes) circular trail to your right which takes you in a loop and back along the River Dane. If you do this, keep to your right all the way round and you will return along the river bank to the Croxton Aqueduct. It is a pleasant diversion and gives you a good view of the aqueduct from below.

14. From the Croxton Aqueduct, continue along the canal. Walk under the A530 at bridge 173. As you come to the outskirts of Middlewich you will pass the point where you very briefly walked along the canal earlier. Soon after this you reach The Big Lock, and *The Big Lock Pub* where you leave the canal and return to your car.

Middlewich

For more detailed information on Middlewich see walk 18.

King Street

See walk 18.

left: Looking back along the Trent and Mersey Canal from The Croxton Aqueduct
right:The Croxton Aqueduct

The Big Lock

The Croxton Aqueduct

The Croxton Aqueduct is made up of riveted cast iron plates which are supported by a girder across the River Dane. It is the third aqueduct on this site, the original one having been completed in the 1770s. You can see the original brick and stone piers from the earlier aqueducts if you look to the left of the present structure. The present aqueduct, built after flooding in the 1930s, was reduced in width to only 8 foot 2 inches. This narrow width restricts the size of boat that can travel between Preston Brook and the centre of Northwich and means there is no benefit in having the wider dimensions at The Big Lock.

In the Autumn of 2012 there was a serious breach here as the result of months of torrential rain. However, unlike at Dutton further north, the repairs took place relatively quickly and the towpath was reopened before the end of the year.

Places you may wish to stop for refreshment

The Big Lock Pub, Middlewich *01606 738354. A modern pub with a wide ranging food menu.*

WALK 18
The Big Lock, Middlewich to Tetton Bridge

The Big Lock – The Trent and Mersey Canal – Tetton Bridge – Bradwall Road – Cledford Lane – Road Beta – King Street – The Big Lock

Starting point	**The Big Lock, Middlewich. Grid reference: 702668**
Length	**6 miles**
Allow	**Approximately 2½ hours**
Map	**OS Explorer 267**
By car	**If coming along the A54 from the east and the M6 Junction 18, go over the canal in the centre of Middlewich, pass the junction with the A533 Sandbach Road then take a right hand filter onto Pepper Street. This is just under 250 yards after the junction and leads you to a short stretch of road with grass either side of it. If coming into Middlewich from the west, you turn left 250 yards before the A533 junction. Once on Pepper Street, turn immediately to the left. Webb's Lane bends to the right and you continue up the road until you see the Big Lock Public House on your right just before a sharp left hand bend. Park near the pub, or in its car park if you intend to stop there on your return**

Both sections of this walk can be divided into two halves. The first stretch along the canal is through Middlewich and includes well landscaped banks and interesting reminders of the past, four pairs of locks, two chandlers and pleasure craft hire. The second canal stretch however runs directly along the side the A533 for about 1¾ miles so perhaps has less to offer to the walker. The first part of the walk back is rural, but later on, the paths go round the edge of Middlewich. Near the end of the walk, take time to read the information board about old Middlewich on King Street. It is a town with a far more interesting past than one might think. Some of the field paths can be muddy so come prepared after wet weather.

The Walk

1. Walk to the right of The Big Lock Pub to reach the towpath and canal which are behind the pub. Turn right. You will walk with the water on your left for almost 2½ miles before leaving the towpath at bridge 165, Tetton Bridge.

2. About ⅓ mile from The Big Lock Pub you pass under bridge 172 which carries the A54. Whilst going under the bridge note the mural which depicts old *Middlewich.* At the other side of the bridge you come to what was once Middlewich Wharf. Along the walk you will see a number of information boards about the town. They are well presented and informative, and you may find them interesting to read.

Middlewich: the chandlery after lock 72

3. You will soon reach Lock 74, the first of the four Middlewich Locks. To your left by lock 73 is the former Seddon's Salt Works site. Between locks 73 and 72, where the canal bends to the right, you will see a dry dock on the far bank. This is where a fleet of narrow boats belonging to Seddons Salt Works were once based. Walk past a small chandlers which is under a covered area on the right then go under bridge 169. Soon you will cross the Middlewich branch of The Shropshire Union Canal. Interestingly, the first few yards of this canal were built by The Trent and Mersey Canal to enable them to collect the tolls.

The junction with the Middlewich branch of The Shropshire Union Canal

4. Pass Kings Lock Chandlery on the opposite bank, behind which is the former site of another

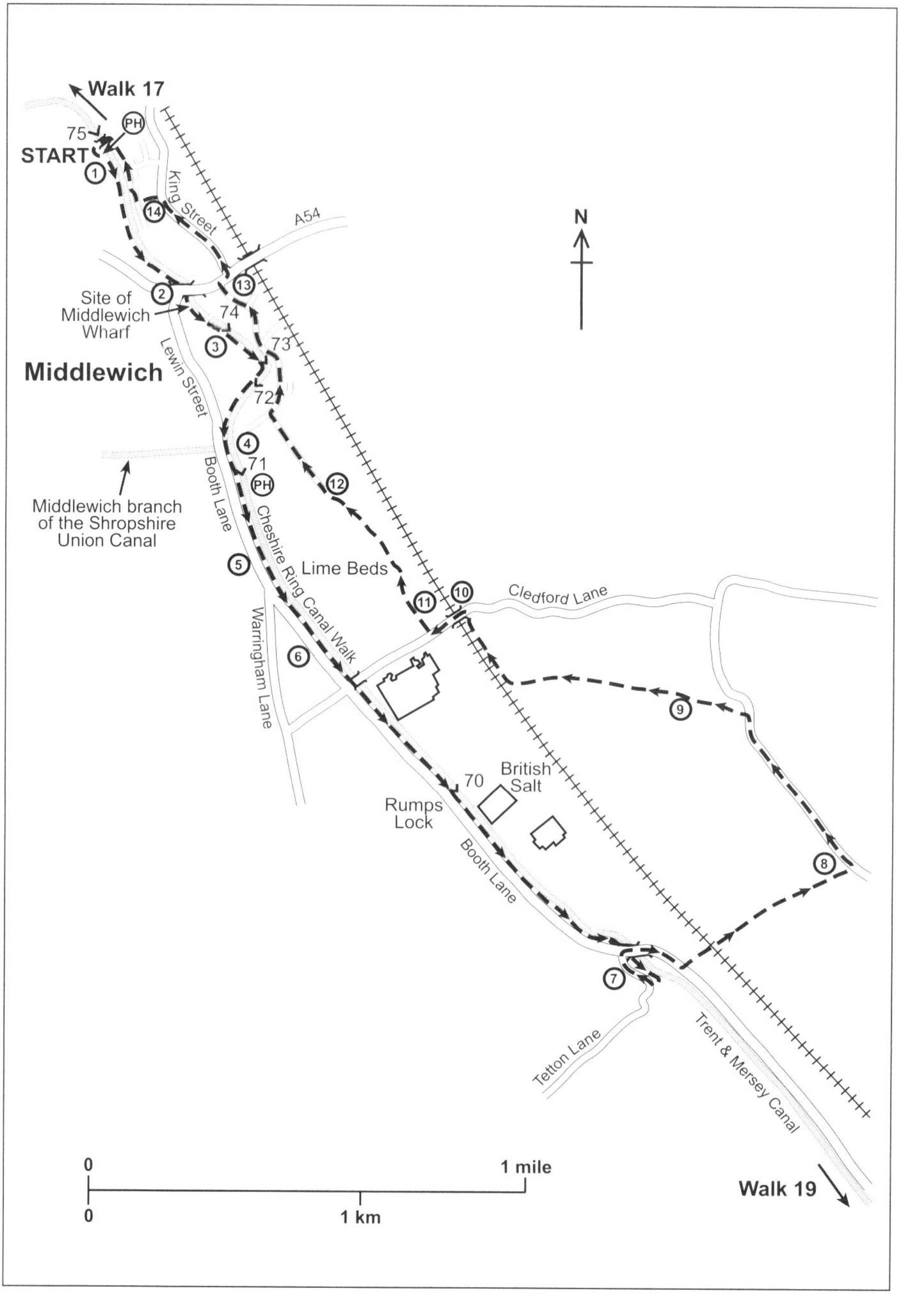

Walk 17
PH
75
START
1
14
King Street
A54
N
2
13
Site of Middlewich Wharf
74
3
73
Middlewich
Lewin Street
72
4
71
PH
Booth Lane
Middlewich branch of the Shropshire Union Canal
12
Cheshire Ring Canal Walk
Lime Beds
5
11
10
Cledford Lane
Warringham Lane
6
9
70
British Salt
Rumps Lock
Booth Lane
8
7
Tetton Lane
Trent & Mersey Canal
0
1 mile
0
1 km
Walk 19

factory belonging to the *Brunner Mond Soda and Bleach Works.* Just past here on your left is *The Kings Lock Public House,* which reopened under new management in 2013/2014. The last of the Middlewich Locks - Lock 71 'The Kings Lock' - is facing the pub.

The Kings Lock Public House and lock 71, the Kings Lock

5. The stretch of canal between here and bridge 165 runs in a relatively straight line alongside the A533. Its saving grace however is the wildlife as swans appear to congregate in this area. On one walk, over 40 swans glided 'en mass' backwards and forwards along the canal, following anyone who

Swans on the canal

they felt might be offering them something to eat. This was quite a sight. It seems however that they do not go hungry as bird seed has frequently been seen here on the canal bank.

6. The A533 is now on your right, and on your left you will see a high bank behind which are lime beds. Once past bridge 166, The Ideal Standard Works, producers of sanitary ware, can be seen on your left, and just after Rump Locks (lock 70) you pass *British Salt.* This is the only surviving salt works in the area and from where over half the United Kingdom's salt once came. Past here on the left is the site of the former RHM factory, but it is now empty and at present is overgrown. You will see a number of similar former industrial sites in the area. You soon come to bridge 165 carrying the A533. Walk under it and a few yards further on leave the canal to your right.

7. At the road turn right. At the A533 turn right again and after about 150 yards you can see a footpath sign over the road on your left, to the right of a gate. Cross the main road with care, go over the stile and follow the track ahead. Walk with the hedge to your right and you soon come to a railway line. You have to cross this directly so do what you are told on the sign, look both ways, shut both gates and proceed with great caution. You then continue in the same direction crossing three fields, and about half a mile after leaving the main road you reach Bradwall Road.

8. Turn left along Bradwall Road and walk for just under ½ mile. After a 'Road narrows' sign and just before a brick bridge you will see a footpath sign to your left which you follow. Go over a small bridge and continue away from the road to the top end of the field. You walk parallel to, but a little way away from a meandering stream which is to your right.

9. Go through a gap into the next large field, then walk ahead, veering slightly left and keeping the stream to your right, continue ahead through a gap with a stile on its right and along an enclosed path. Just before a railway line and about ½ mile after leaving the road, turn right to walk with the railway on your left for about 350 yards to reach Cledford Lane.

10. At Cledford Lane turn left, and walk under the railway line. In a little over 150 yards you will see a footpath sign on your right which you follow. This is just before some green railings and raised industrial land ahead right and opposite green railings on the left.

11. Turn right to walk along this path for almost ½ mile, at first following the raised area, which is now on your left. Behind this are the lime beds you could see from the canal side. You now walk through a former industrial area, which in parts looks empty and neglected, although the path you follow is wide, enclosed and well maintained. Keep ahead, past a gate on your left which leads to views of the lime beds, after which the path narrow slightly, then bends left and right to reach a high wire gate with a gap on its right. Go through the gap.

12. Walk along a short stretch of road, past what is at present a Volvo dealer on your right and through an open gate across the road. If the gate happens to be closed, go through the small gap on the left onto Road Beta. Walk down Road Beta, passing small industry on either side, to reach Brooks Lane in about 250 yards. Here you turn right. You now walk along the road through an industrial area for about ⅓ mile before reaching the A54. To the left is the *Boars Head Hotel.*

13. Turn right at the A54, cross the main road with care, continue in the same direction for a few more yards then turn left into *King Street.* Walk along here for about ¼ mile, noting the information board about *Roman Middlewich.* There is more to this town than you might have thought and it is worth stopping to read this notice. Where the road bears slightly to the right, go down Webb Lane on your left. This is easy to miss and is by a post box on a wall. Webb Lane leads you down past some houses onto Hadrians Way.

14. Turn right at Hadrians Way and after a few yards take a footpath down to your left which you will continue along in the same direction. To your left is a wide stream, and behind that is the canal. After about 250 yards, turn left to go over the stream and then over the canal bridge. You are above lock 75 'The Big Lock', so note its wide dimensions. Turn left and within a few yards come to The Big Lock Pub, after which you will turn right to return to your car.

Footbridge over the Trent and Mersey Canal by the Big Lock

There are some information boards between The Big Lock Pub and the canal which you may find of interest.

King Street and The Romans in Middlewich

In 48 AD the Romans set up a temporary camp in Middlewich and in 70 AD the first permanent Roman fort was built. King Street was a major Roman road and it linked the area with more northern parts of Britain. The town grew as a result of its salt deposits and by 300 AD Middlewich had established itself as a crossroads. Around 350 AD the Middlewich salt workings came under church control. The Romans left Britain between 400 AD and 450 AD.

Middlewich and the salt industry

Since Roman times, Middlewich has been a salt making town. By Anglo Saxon times most of the salt works were north of the town, to the west of the river Croco. In the 17th century, iron pans and also pumps to bring the brine out of the ground were introduced.

The building of the Trent and Mersey Canal was fully supported by salt work owners in the town as the only way at the time of transporting the salt was on very poor roads. By 1776 five out of the six Middlewich salt works were connected to the canal network. The salt industry remained important throughout the Victorian times and both Saxa Salt and Bisto were manufactured here well into the 20th century.

The growth of the chemical industry in the area led to the decline of traditional salt works and technical advances resulted in the merger of the bigger companies. The only surviving salt works in operation today is British Salt.

Present day Middlewich

Today Middlewich is a busy centre for pleasure craft, having two hire fleets, a boat yard and two chandleries. The town is at the junction of The Trent and Mersey Canal and The Middlewich Branch of The Shropshire Union Canal so connects The Cheshire Ring and beyond (including the River Weaver) with Nantwich and Chester. There is a lot of activity in the Summer so be glad when you are able to walk past all the boats as they queue to pass through the locks on busy weekends and holidays.

Middlewich Wharf

Middlewich became a significant trading town, as the result of the building of The Trent and Mersey Canal, and with the subsequent construction of the Middlewich Branch of the Shropshire Union canal it became an important junction. Many large company carriers and also smaller independent carriers were based in the wharf area just to the south of the A54. Goods such as food and building materials were brought in by boat, and salt and coal were taken out. Apparently, however, according to one of the information boards, cheese was the biggest export from here, being taken by canal boat to many parts of the country! In the past, the offices of the Trent and Mersey Canal Company were located on the wharf in a building which can still be seen slightly back from the canal. The offices of agents for the North Staffordshire Railway and Canal Company and the Shropshire Union Canal Company were also located here, as were company offices for a number of merchants who worked in the wharf area.

Brunner Mond

See walk 13.

British Salt

British Salt was purchased by Tata Chemicals (formerly known as Brunner Mond) in 2010. At the time of writing about 125 people are employed here and they produce approximately 800,000 tonnes of white salt a year. It is said (though the author cannot verify this) that its 'salt mountain' can be seen from Booth Lane.

Places you may wish to stop for refreshment

The Big Lock Pub: *01606 738354. See walk 17.*

The Kings Lock Pub: *01606 836894. A traditional canal side pub which has recently been sympathetically refurbished. The service is friendly and helpful and the food is traditional with interesting twists. Dogs are welcome and dog biscuits provided!*

The Boars Head Hotel: *01606 833191*

www.robinsonsbrewery.com/boarshead

A pub with an interesting traditional interior.

WALK 19
Tetton Bridge to Elworth

Elworth – Moston - Tetton Bridge - The Trent and Mersey Canal - Elworth

Starting point	**By the canal near Elworth, off the A533 Middlwich to Sandbach road. Grid reference: 733611**
Length	**5 miles**
Allow	**Approximately 2 hours**
Map	**OS Explorer 267**
By car	**From the A533 in Elworth, turn south west down Moss Lane. This is just north of Sandbach Station, between the bridge over the railway line and The Fox Pub. Ignore any side roads that lead to houses, and stay on Moss Lane as it bends to the left then to the right. After this, continue ahead to cross over the canal bridge. Park immediately after the bridge in a small car park to your left, or if this is full, somewhere nearby**

This is an undemanding, varied walk through the rural Cheshire Plain. Note the many flashes which are now fishing lakes. There are two shorter and one longer section of road, but these are quiet with little traffic. On the canal you pass 3 locks, and the surroundings are pleasant, although as on walk 18, the A533 runs alongside for a short stretch. Unfortunately there are no refreshment opportunities on the walk, but after completion there are a number of pubs, coffee shops and restaurants in nearby Sandbach and the surrounding area. Parts of the walk can get muddy after wet weather.

The Walk

1. With your back to the canal, keep right to walk along Oakwood Lane. The road bears right and about 125 yards after the bend you come to a private fishing lake on your left. At the far end of the lake, take a footpath immediately to your left which goes across the top of the lake and into

some woods. Take the right hand track, not the one leading to the lakeside.

Private fishing lake

2. Continue along this track through Moat Nature Reserve. This may be wet at the start, but does become drier as you go along. Although the path may be overgrown in places, it is an obvious way through and you soon come to Plant Lane. At Plant Lane turn right, pass a black and white house on your right and a field gate on your left, and in less than 100 yards turn left to follow a sign up some steps and through a gate by a large tree.

3. Walk ahead with the hedge to your right in the first field, go over a stile and follow the sign across the next field. You are making for a stile in a corner of the field which is ahead and slightly to the right of three trees in the far hedge. The sign which points slightly diagonally left may confuse you. When you have crossed the stile into the third field, follow the sign which tells you to bear right and you soon reach Green Lane. Here you turn left.

4. Green Lane crosses over the bottom of a long narrow lake. About ¼ mile after joining the lane, and almost immediately after a house on your right, you can see a footpath sign and stile to your right, which you follow. You now walk due north. After a while the path becomes a track. Continue ahead along what is still a right of way, even though you have to go through some gates across the driveway. Pass Fields Farm on your right and about ½ mile after leaving Green Lane you reach Dragons Lane

5. Turn right at Dragons Lane. The road dips down, and just before you come to some more water, turn left through a metal gate. You now walk with a lake on your right. After about 150 yards, go through another metal gate. Do not now turn right to cross over the lake, nor ahead left, but continue ahead on a path along the lakeside which is ahead right from the gate. If you look carefully you will see the sign directing you along the left hand side of the lake.

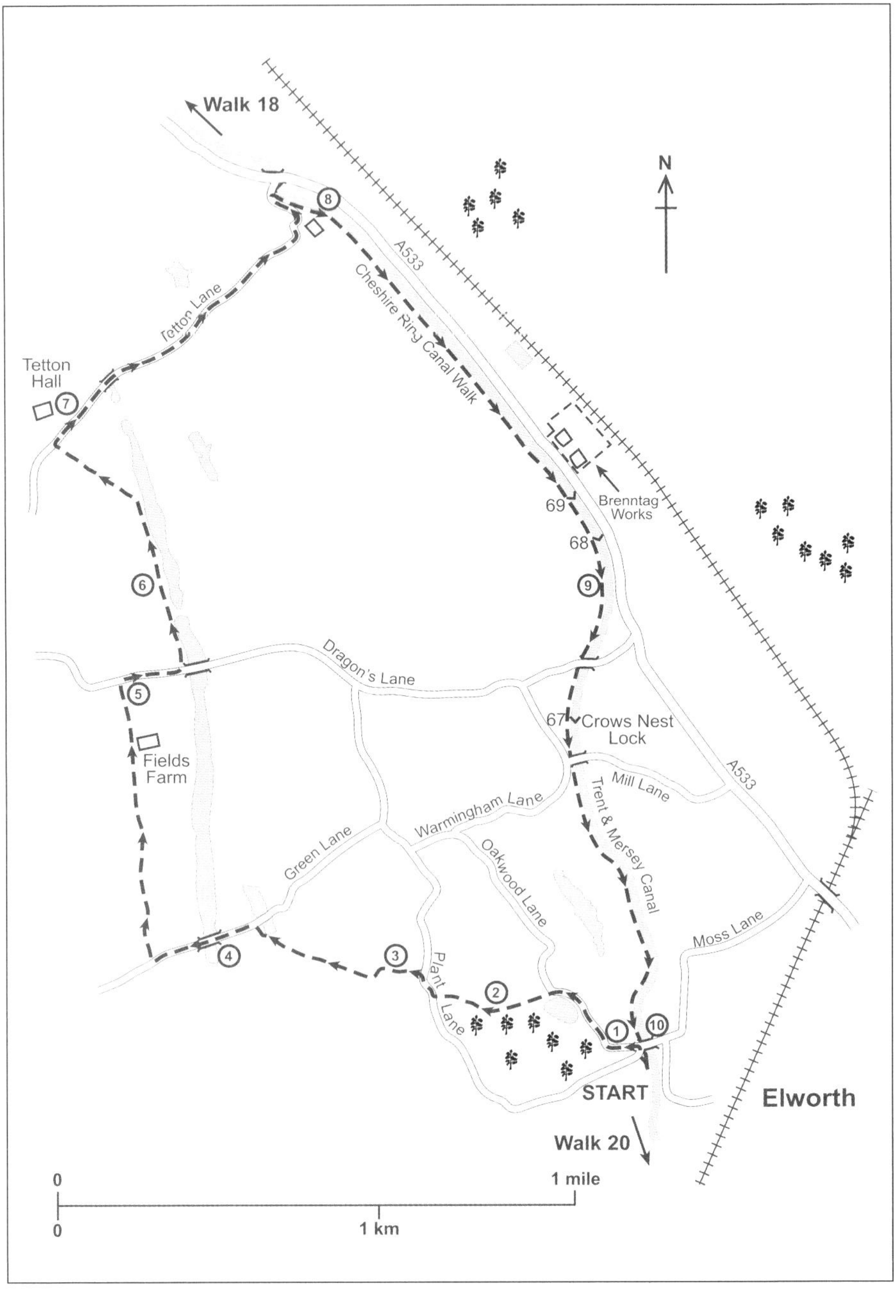

Walk 18
N
A533
Cheshire Ring Canal Walk
Tetton Lane
Tetton Hall
Brenntag Works
69
68
Dragon's Lane
Crows Nest Lock
67
Fields Farm
Mill Lane
Trent & Mersey Canal
Warmingham Lane
Oakwood Lane
Green Lane
Plant Lane
Moss Lane
START
Elworth
Walk 20
0
1 mile
0
1 km

6. Walk ahead keeping the lake to your right and trees to your left. Cross another stile and continue to stay close to the lake. After the next stile, the path veers to the left, and you cross this field diagonally, to reach Tetton Lane by some small stables.

Fishing lake – the footpath is on the left hand side

7. Turn right down Tetton Lane, passing Tetton Hall on your left. Walk along here for about ¾ mile, noting yet again, the fishing lake on the right. Just after passing a large house with interesting chimneys to your right, the road bears left. In less than 50 yards past the bend, go through a gap in the hedge on your right to join the canal towpath, and turn right again.

Brenntag Works

8. You will walk along the canal with the water on your left for approximately 2 miles, passing the three Booth Lane Locks before leaving at bridge 160. The first mile follows the busy A533 on the opposite bank, which cannot be avoided. After about ½ mile pass lock 69. Note the overflow channel and rill to the right of this and the other two locks. Just before lock 69, you can see the large Brenntag Works,, a chemical blending plant. This, along with a new housing development, is on the large site of the former Albion Chemical Works.

9. Soon after the middle lock, no. 68, you will notice the main road veers away to the left. There is a small business park on the left, after which the walk becomes quieter and more rural. Pass Crows Nest Lock (lock 67) and bridge 161 then note a number of boats moored on the far side of

Lock 68

the canal. These are soon followed by an interesting grassed garden area with benches, also on the far side of the canal.

10. About a mile after the main road leaves the canal side, and about ⅔ mile after the third lock, you pass two houses on the right. Walk under bridge 160, the metal Elton Moss Bridge and leave the towpath through the small car park on the right, to return to your car.

Places you may wish to stop for refreshment

There are no places to stop for refreshment along the route, but the following are not far away:

The Bear's Paw, Warmington: 01270 526317 **www.thebearspaw.co.uk**
A food orientated pub about 10 minutes drive away. Recommended.
Sandbach: *There are a number of food and drink establishments in Sandbach.*

WALK 20
Elworth to Wheelock

Elworth – The Trent and Mersey Canal – Wheelock – Fields Farm – Elton Flashes – Watch Lane Flash – Elworth

Starting point	**By the canal near Elworth, off the A533 Middlwich to Sandbach road. Grid reference: 733611**
Length	**6½ miles**
Allow	**Approximately 2½-3 hours**
Maps	**OS Explorer 267 and OS Explorer 257**
By car	**From the A533 in Elworth, turn south west down Moss Lane. This is just north of Sandbach Station, between the bridge over the railway line and The Fox Pub. Ignore any side roads that lead to houses, and stay on Moss Lane as it bends to the left and then to the right. After this, continue ahead to cross over the canal bridge. Park immediately after the bridge in a small car park to your left, or if this is full, somewhere nearby,**

Apart from the short middle section of road in Wheelock, this walk is through fields and along mainly quiet lanes. Although it is not a difficult walk, it can be slow going across the fields as in the summer the grass can grow quite high, parts of the ground can be uneven and the path does not seem to be well used. You may wish to wear long trousers and stout footwear. However, the footpath signs are there if you look for them and the stiles and kissing gates are well maintained. Both Elton Flashes and Watch Lane Flash near the end of the walk attract much interesting wildfowl.

The Walk

1. Walk ahead through the little car park to the towpath where you turn right. You will walk with the water to your left for slightly under 2½ miles before leaving the canal at Bridge 154 in Wheelock. The canal soon

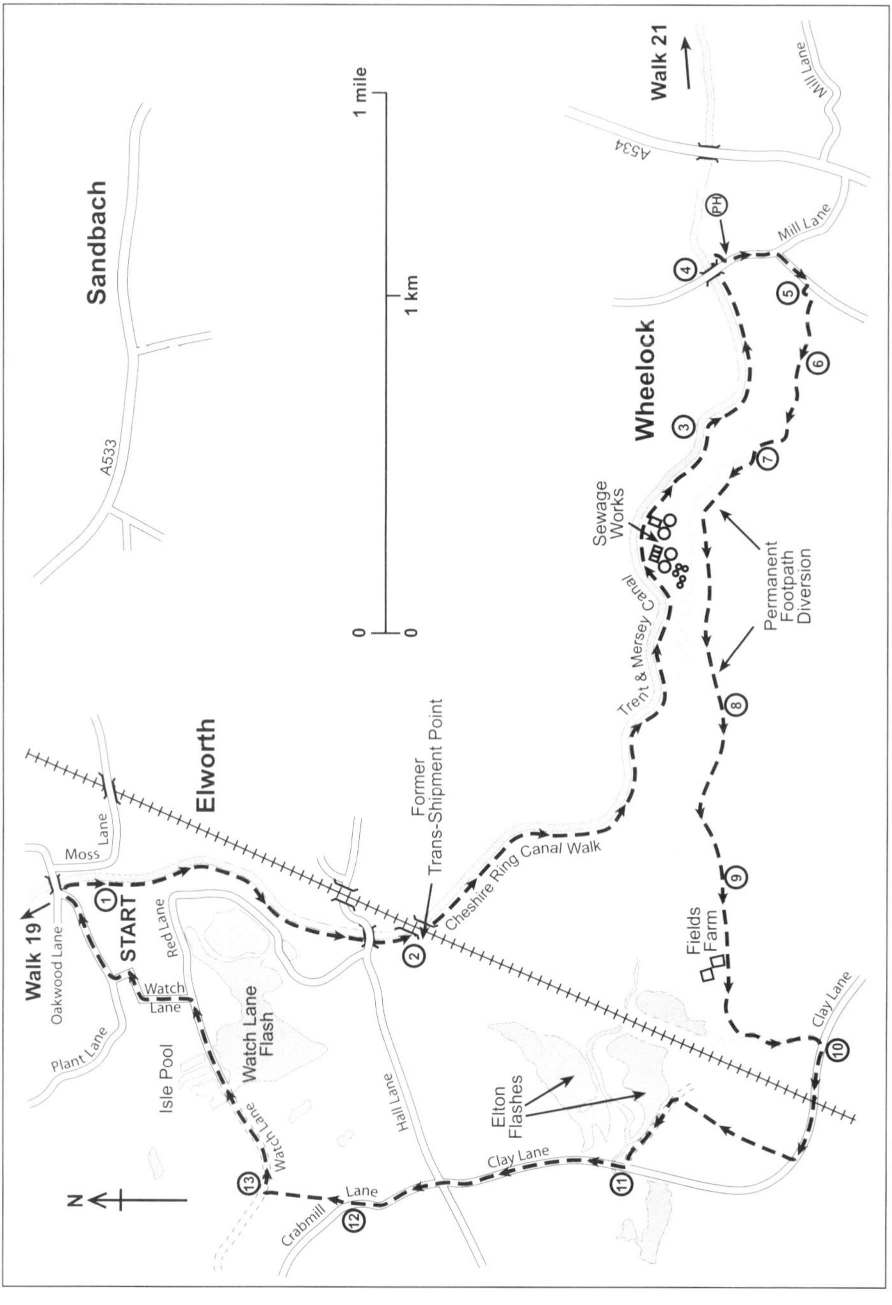
Sandbach
A533
1 mile
1 km
0
0
Walk 21
Mill Lane
A534
PH
Mill Lane
Wheelock
Sewage Works
Trent & Mersey Canal
Permanent Footpath Diversion
Elworth
Former Trans-Shipment Point
Cheshire Ring Canal Walk
Moss Lane
Walk 19
START
Oakwood Lane
Red Lane
Watch Lane
Plant Lane
Isle Pool
Watch Lane Flash
Hall Lane
Elton Flashes
Fields Farm
Clay Lane
Clay Lane
Crabmill Lane
Watch Lane
N
1
2
3
4
5
6
7
8
9
10
11
12
13

bears round to the right. Down to your right you can see *Watch Lane Flash*, and a new housing estate has been recently built on the left between bridges 158 and 159. Note the reinforced bank here and along much of the canal up to Wheelock. This has been made necessary because of local subsidence in the area.

2. About ¾ mile after joining the canal and just after bridge 159, the mainline Manchester to Crewe railway crosses the canal at *Ettily Heath*. *Sandbach* is a mile to your left. After this, the canal meanders through open countryside. Soon after bridge 157 you can see a wire fence on the right and behind it a reasonably well hidden sewage works. Past bridge 156 the canal becomes more enclosed and houses can be seen.

The canal leading to open countryside between Elworth and Wheelock

The more enclosed towpath between Elworth and Wheelock

3. The houses continue by the canal on your left as you enter the outskirts of *Wheelock* and after bridge 155 there are some attractive gardens which back on to the canal. At the bottom of one, two swans have been seen nesting with their two cygnets. Slightly over ¼ mile further on and just before bridge 154, there is a gate across the towpath which you walk round. Once under bridge 154, walk past an old warehouse on your right – at present housing an Italian restaurant.

4. Immediately after the old warehouse you come to Wheelock Quay. Turn right here to leave the canal. Turn right again to walk round the building and through a small car park to reach the road where you turn left. Cross over the road as soon as possible, remembering to take care. Continue along the pavement as the road bears to the right. After passing some cottages

which are slightly set back from the road, you come to Brooks Farm on your right. Walk past the next field, then just before some houses on the right, turn right to follow a footpath sign.

Wheelock Wharf

5. Walk along a short track with houses on your left, then go through a gate ahead. Continue across the corner of a field towards another gate which is to the left of Brooks Farm. Go through the gate and turn left onto a track. The farm buildings and yard will now be behind you and a large cowshed to your right.

6. Throughout the next section until you reach the lane to Fields Farm you will be following the direction of the River Wheelock which will be over to your right. Continue ahead along the track and after about ¼ mile you will see a footpath sign pointing to the right over a grassy area, which you follow. Look carefully for this sign as it is quite easy to miss, and indicates you are to go ahead right just after a farm gate across the track, which is usually left open. Cross the grass diagonally (or if it is too long in the summer go beside the far hedge) and just before reaching the river bank, bear left through a wide gap between hedges. The River Wheelock is immediately to your right at this point.

7. Keeping the hedge on your left continue ahead and go through a new kissing gate. Carry on in the same direction across a long narrow field, passing a tree in the centre, to another kissing gate at the far side. The ground can be uneven, and as the footpath appears to be little used, the grass may be high in mid summer. As a result the walking may be slow at times, but the signs are there if you look for them. Continue ahead through the gate and across the next field keeping parallel to the River Wheelock at first, but then veering towards it and a towards large tree which is ahead right. The tree is near the far right corner of the field and by a small stream.

8. At the narrow point of the field, look to your left and you will see the sign directing you left over a bridge across a small stream. Turn left to cross

the bridge then turn immediately right. Walk along the edge of the field with the hedge on your right, go through a gate at the right hand corner of this field and keep to the right round the next field. Walk through another gate and go diagonally across the next field as indicated on the sign. You are crossing towards a large tree, which is in a row of vegetation alongside a dip in the field. When you get close to the tree you will see a wooden bridge which takes you over a small stream. Cross the bridge and walk ahead to a gate by a tree, leading to a track.

9. Turn right along the track to pass Fields Farm on your right. Continue ahead for a short while, then after the farm bear left, ignoring another track that joins from the right. When you come to a crossing track leading to the railway line on your right, turn left. Pass two attractive small flashes on either side, to join a road.

10. Turn right here, go under the railway bridge, and shortly you see footpath signs to both the left and right. Take the one to the right to go up some steps which can be overgrown in the summer. Go through a gate into a field, taking care after wet weather as it may be muddy. Walk directly across the field and at the other side go through a gate to join a track. Turn left, and in slightly under 350 yards you come to Clay Lane.

11. Turn right and walk along Clay Lane passing *Elton Flashes Nature Reserve* to your right. Here, you may be able to walk down a path on your right in order to get a clearer view of the wildfowl on the Flash. However, you must then retrace your steps to the Clay Lane. About ⅓ mile after joining Clay Lane you reach a cross roads. Proceed across Hall Lane with care and continue ahead along the quieter Crabmill Lane.

12. After about ¼ mile and where the road bears to the left, go over a stile by a gate on the right, following some footpath signs. Once over, follow the smaller yellow sign for the more minor path which bears left, and not the sign indicating ahead. After a few yards turn left to go round a tree. Continue in this direction keeping the edge of the field on your left. In the far left field corner there is a part hidden stile onto Watch Lane.

13. Cross the stile and turn right onto what is at first a dirt track. As it becomes a metalled road you can see *Watch Lane Flash* on your right and the delightful Isle Pool on your left. Walk past the flashes and about ⅓ mile after turning into Watch Lane come to a road to your left, still called Watch

Lane where you turn left. The road bends right and left to reach Plant Lane. Turn right here, and in about 350 yards, you will see the canal and car park ahead, and return to your car.

The Isle Pool

Watch Lane Flash and Elton Flashes

Elton Flashes and Watch Lane Flash are typical Cheshire Flashes. Flashes were formed when underground caverns collapsed, as a result of salt in the form of brine being pumped from them. They are now nature reserves and attract many types of wildfowl.

Ettily Heath

This was once a trans shipment point between canal and rail, for goods going to and coming from The Potteries. In this area you may notice the bank is reinforced with steel piles and concrete as the canal here is deeper in some sections due to past subsidence related to salt mining.

Sandbach

Sandbach is a pleasant market town despite the nearby salt industry. The two Saxon stone crosses in the cobbled market place are believed to date from the 7th century, built to commemorate the conversion of the area to Christianity. They were broken up and scattered by Puritans in the 17th century, but after many years of searching were rebuilt and re-erected in 1816.

Wheelock

Wheelock is named after the River Wheelock which in turn derived its name from an old Welsh word meaning 'winding river'. It is a very old village as it was named in the Domesday Book as Quelock. Its location, where The Trent and Mersey Canal crossed the Sandback to Crewe Road, resulted in its growth as a thriving canalside community.

Places you may wish to stop for refreshment

The Cheshire Cheese, Wheelock: *01270 346600*

An unpretentious pub which serves good wholesome food, with friendly welcoming service. There is a garden at the back in for use in summer.

WALK 21

Wheelock to Hassall Green

Wheelock – The Trent and Mersey Canal – Hassall Green – Cold Moss Heath – Wheelock

Starting point	**By the canal in Wheelock.Grid reference: 751592**
Length	**5 miles**
Allow	**Approximately 2 hours**
Map	**OS Explorer 268**
By car	**Wheelock is south of Sandbach just off the A534 Sandbach to Crewe Road. Park if you can in the small car park opposite the Cheshire Cheese Pub and Wheelock Wharf. If this is full, it is suggested you park on Forge Fields 100 yards north, then cross the main road, walk back over the canal and turn left to start the walk at Wheelock Wharf**

The ascent of *The Cheshire Flight or 'Heartbreak Hill'* begins at Wheelock and as a result the canal section on this and walks 22 and 23 is arguably the most interesting stretch of The Trent and Mersey Canal on The Cheshire Ring. There are 26 locks in the 6½ miles between Wheelock and Hardings Wood Junction, most of which are 'paired' locks. This walk contains nine of the locks, these being the eight locks in The Wheelock Flight (locks 66 to 59) plus lock 58 just before Hassall Green. Apart from two short road sections, the return is across fields, along a delightful wooded valley and past an interesting arboretum.

The Walk

1. From the car park by the canal at bridge 154 in the centre of *Wheelock*, walk across what was once Wheelock Wharf onto the towpath. Turn right and you will walk in an easterly direction with the water on your left for just under 2 miles to leave the canal at bridge 147 in Hassall Green. Note

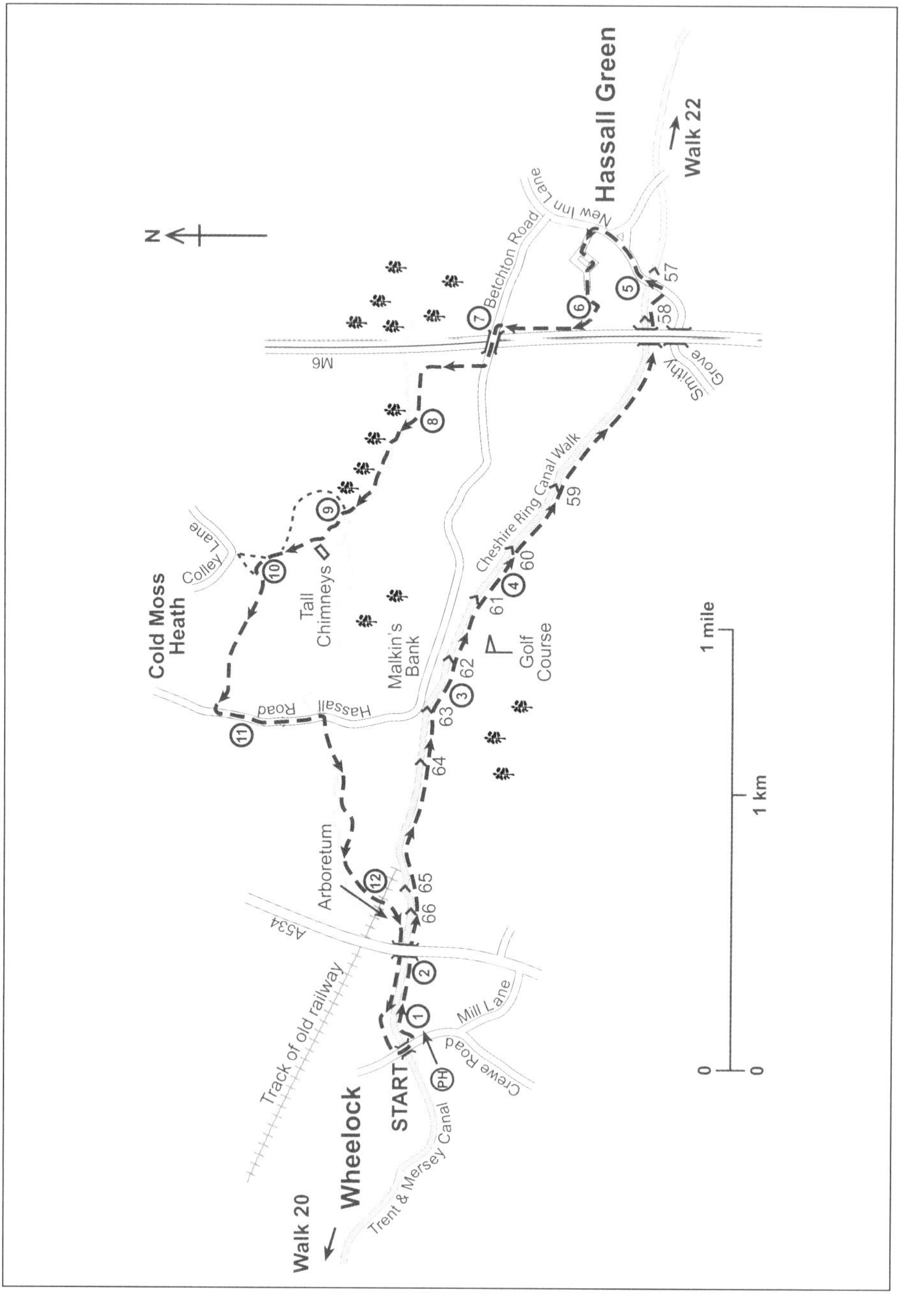
Hassall Green
Walk 22
New Inn Lane
Betchton Road
N
M6
Smithy Grove
Cheshire Ring Canal Walk
Cold Moss Heath
Colley Lane
Tall Chimneys
Malkin's Bank
Golf Course
Hassall Road
Arboretum
A534
Track of old railway
Wheelock
START
PH
Mill Lane
Crewe Road
Trent & Mersey Canal
Walk 20
1 mile
1 km
0
0
1
2
3
4
5
6
7
8
9
10
11
12
57
58
59
60
61
62
63
64
65
66

that at Wheelock there is a short towpath on the northern side of the canal which you do not go onto until your return.

2. Walk away from Wheelock and under the A534, then walk past lock 66 followed by lock 65, both of which were refurbished and reopened as paired locks in 2010 and 2012 respectively. One of each of these pairs had been closed 'temporarily' in the 1960s. Once you have passed lock 64 you will come to *Malkin's Bank*, a canal side village with both new and older terraced houses, one of which used to be the boatman's co-op.

Lock 64

Malkin's Bank from Lock 63

3. Walk past lock 63 in Malkin's Bank, then beside some cottages on your right. Go over a side bridge carrying the towpath over an old arm of the canal which once led to one of the many factories belonging to the former *Brunner Mond Chemical Works*. This factory occupied the land to your right, which has since been reclaimed and is now used as a golf course. Almost immediately after this you come to lock 62, which at the time of writing must pose a dilemma to boaters. This is because there is a steep weir inside the near lock, but there is no clear sign telling them it is not in use.

4. Continue up past locks 61 to 59, after which you will begin to get good views ahead to your left. Bridge 148 is interesting as it seems to be a very large structure to carry what appears to be a very minor footpath! Almost immediately after this the canal passes under the M6 motorway bridge. Once past Lock 58, come up off the canal to your right as you reach bridge 147. Turn left at the road to cross the canal. On the right, by lock 57, there was until recently a very pleasant café/restaurant and also a convenience

Lock 62 with weir at one side

store but unfortunately they closed around the end of 2012. Note the well landscaped area around lock 57.

5. Once over the bridge, continue ahead. Walk past two lanes on your right and the new development of The Paddock on your left and in just over 300 yards after leaving the canal turn left into Charles Square. Walk down here and take the first left so the square and children's playground are on your right. Walk round two sides of the square. When you get to the opposite corner from where you entered the square, bear left down a short cul de sac and walk down the footpath which is between bungalows number 55 and 57 in the corner.

6. This footpath bends left then right along the field boundary and you walk round the left hand side of the large field to soon come to the motorway. Bear right to walk with the motorway on your left and cross into another field. At the far side of this field, go through a gate, turn right to go through another gate and you will reach Betchton Road.

7. Turn left at the road, cross over the motorway and you soon come to a footpath sign and stile on the right. Turn right to go over the stile and then over another stile almost immediately. Walk directly across the field and at the far side cross a third stile. However note that the field boundaries here may only be temporary. Once over, bear diagonally left over what at the time

of writing is a grassy field, to reach a small stretch of woodland at the back of the field. Here you turn left and walk with the woodland on your right.

8. Continue for a few yards until the path leads you down to the right through light woodland to a footbridge. Cross the footbridge then bear left to follow the meandering stream which is on your left. This is a well waymarked, delightful little valley, full of wild flowers in the spring including English wood anemones. You would have no idea that the M6 is less than half a mile away! Continue to follow the stream for about ¼ mile until you reach Stannerhouse Lane, though you may have to go up to your right at one point to avoid some mud.

9. Go directly across Stannerhouse Lane, keeping the bridge and stream on your left. Follow the path which leads slightly to the right, away from the stream and up to, and around 'Tall Chimneys', a large house which you keep to your left. Walk along the well marked path, as it leads you into an open field past the house. Continue in the same direction towards a large tree in the middle of the field ahead of you. Once past the tree, make for the far left corner of the field.

10. Go through a gate and cross directly over the drive leading to 'Tall Chimneys'. Go through the gate opposite and straight across a small field to go through a third gate. Here you turn left, then bear right to follow round the left hand side of the field, keeping Vicarage Farm at first to your left and then behind you. You are making for the buildings of Cold Moss Heath in the distance. Descend to cross a bridge across a stream, then up some steps and ahead left over grass, keeping a hedge and houses on your right. When you come to a track, bear right to reach Hassall Road in Cold Moss Heath.

11. At the road turn left. After about ⅓ mile you come to a footpath sign on the right which you follow. This footpath leads you by a meandering stream which you keep to your right. About ⅓ mile after leaving the road you can see a tree ahead with a telegraph pole to its left, and further up to the left is a stile which you cross over. Follow the sign to go up diagonally left and the path leads you down to a tunnel under a disused railway line.

12. Go under the tunnel and walk past an attractive small arboretum on your left. Continue ahead right and note that there are also young trees being grown to the right of the path. After passing a cottage on your left, you

reach the canal. Do not cross over the bridge to the main towpath, but continue ahead right and follow a path that leads along the other bank, with the water to your left. Walk under the A534 and stay by the canal for about ¼ mile all the way back to Wheelock and your car.

Wheelock

See walk 20.

The Brunner Mond Chemical Works

See walk 13.

Malkin's Bank

This settlement was once home to the families of boatmen who worked short haul journeys connected to the salt and chemical industries. There is a good mix of old cottages and well designed modern dwellings. The area to the south of the canal which is now occupied by a golf club house and car park was once the site of a factory belonging to Brunner Mond Chemical Works. The short canal arm where goods were once loaded onto canal boats is now used as a boatyard where traditional working boats are restored.

The Cheshire Flight or 'Heartbreak Hill'

This ascent of 250 feet in 6½ miles is often known to boaters as 'Heartbreak Hill' as there are 26 locks between Wheelock and Hardings Wood Junction. They were originally built as single locks by Telford but by the 1830s, traffic on the canal was so heavy that they were replaced by ones designed by Brindley. He duplicated all the locks except locks 55 and 56 The Pierpoint Locks, so reducing the time it took to pass through them. Due to various factors, some are no longer paired locks, and those that remain are no longer always used as they were intended. However, they still provide interest for the walker.

The Wheelock Flight

The Wheelock Flight of eight paired locks is the most northerly group of locks in the Cheshire Flight.

Places you may wish to stop for refreshment

The Cheshire Cheese, Wheelock: *01270 346600. See walk 20.*

WALK 22
Hassall Green to Rode Heath

Hassall Green – The Trent and Mersey Canal – Thurlwood/Rode Heath – Lawton Heath – The Salt Line – Hassall Green

Starting point	**The Salt Line car park near Hassall Green. Grid reference: 775582**
Length	**5 miles**
Allow	**1¾-2 hours**
Map	**OS Explorer 268**
By car	**Turn south off the A533 towards Hassall Green about 2 miles south east of Sandbach. When you reach Hassall Green, cross the canal, bear right by the little church, then go under the motorway and bear left. Park in the Salt Line car park which is on your right**

This is a fast, easy walk, and although for a walk of this length it would normally take 2 hours plus, it can easily be walked more quickly. Unless the weather is wet or icy, there is probably no need for walking boots. The canal section is interesting as you pass a number of locks and walk through pleasant countryside and the well landscaped edge of Thurlwood/Rode Heath. The return section along the road and The Salt Line is quiet, easy walking.

The walk

1. Return to the road from the car park. On the opposite side of the road, note a house that appears to have once been the station for the *Salt Line* Railway. Turn left and follow the road round for ¼ mile, walking under the motorway and back to the canal in Hassall Green. Walk over the bridge then turn right towards the canal side and cross back over lock 57, which was originally a paired lock. Turn left on the towpath and you will walk with the water to your left for approximately 2¼ miles to leave at bridge 139.

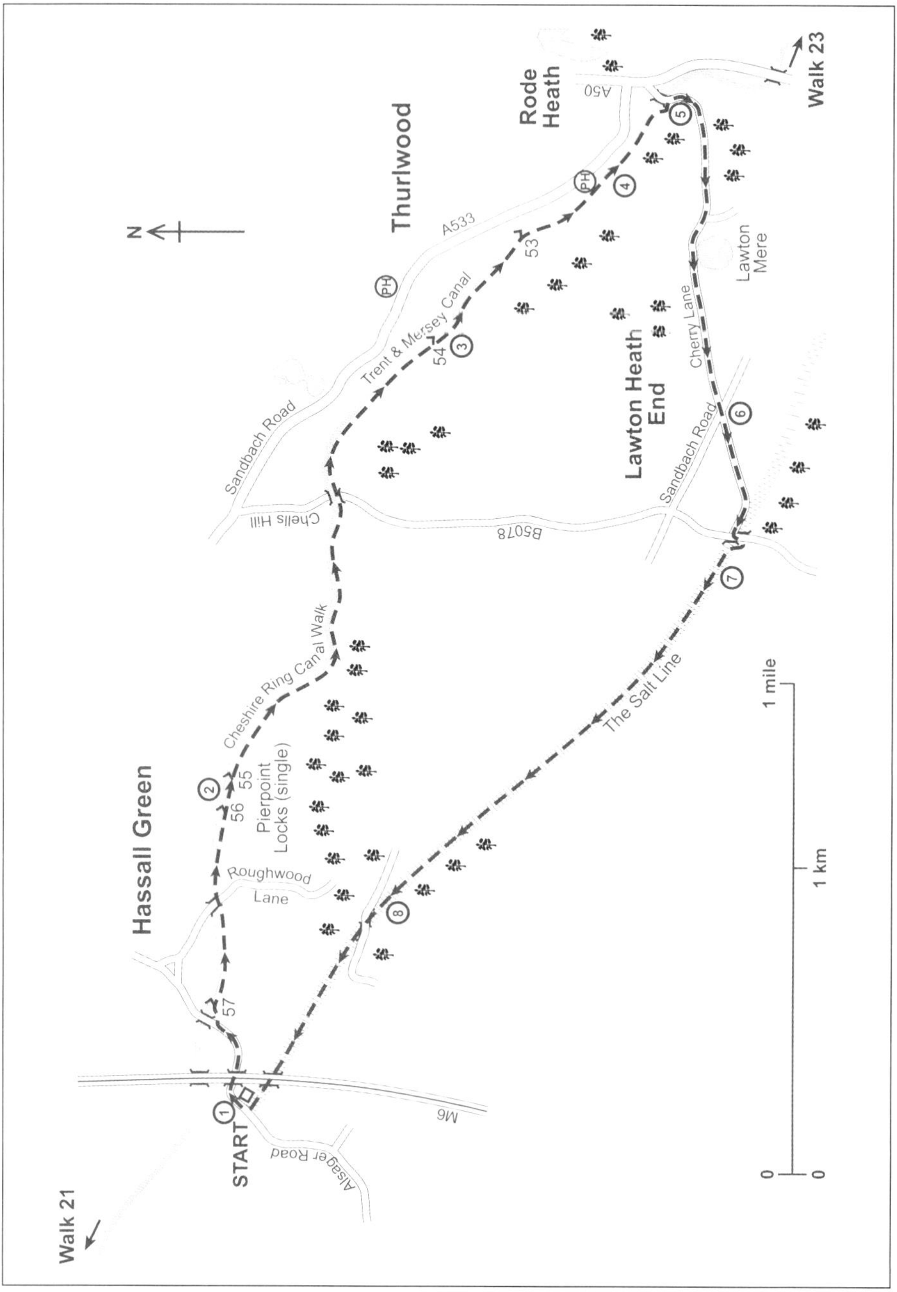

N
Hassall Green
Thurlwood
Rode Heath
Lawton Heath End
Lawton Mere
START
Walk 21
Walk 23
M6
Alsager Road
Roughwood Lane
Pierpoint Locks (single)
Cheshire Ring Canal Walk
Trent & Mersey Canal
Sandbach Road
Chells Hill
B5078
A533
A50
PH
Cherry Lane
The Salt Line
57
56
55
54
53
1
2
3
4
5
6
7
8
0
1 km
1 mile

2. After ½ mile, you pass locks 56 and 55, The Pierpoint Locks, the only two locks in the Cheshire Flight which were not converted to paired locks in the 1830s. On this stretch you will continue up '*Heartbreak Hill*' and as you ascend towards the higher ground you are able to see Mow Cop and the surrounding hills more clearly ahead. Walk past a number of moored boats, noting some old winding gear to your right on the towpath. Soon after crossing Chells Aqueduct on bridge 143, you come to bridge 142 and immediately after this bridge you pass lock 54, another imposing pair of locks.

3. After lock 54 and about 1½ miles after leaving Hassall Green you reach *Thurlwood and Rode Heath.* Here there are a variety of houses backing onto the canal including both old cottages and more modern houses, designed to make the most of their canal side location. At lock 53, go up some steep steps or alternatively round to the right to return back to the canal. This lock was rebuilt as a single lock in 1958 because it had sunk as a result of salt mining subsidence.

4. Slightly further on by bridge 140 you will come to *The Broughton Arms Public House* on your left. This has a pleasant terrace siding onto the canal and is a good place for a drink, snack or lunch either during or after the walk. The canal leaves Rode Heath and soon you reach the flat Bridge 139. Just before the bridge, go up to your right to leave the towpath and join Cherry Lane.

Winding gear by the canal

Lock 53, Rode Heath

5. Turn right along Cherry Lane, away from its junction with the busy A50. The lane bears to the right. Pass a lane which joins from the left, followed by Lawton Mere and about half a mile after this you come to a cross roads. Cross Sandbach Road to continue along Cherry Lane, but take care, as the traffic goes past at some speed.

6. Continue along Cherry Lane. You pass some houses on your right and soon come to a 'No Entry' sign for cars, which as a pedestrian you ignore and simply continue in the same direction. About 250 yards after the 'No Entry' sign you reach another road. Cross the road and slightly to the left is the start of '*The Salt Line'* which is the track of an old railway.

7. You will walk ahead along the Salt Line for 1½ miles. It is a clear, wide path and easy walking, but take care because further along the trail you are warned of rabbit holes if you wander off the track! There are a number of footpaths to the left including one to a 'Tree Trail and Borrow Pit Meadows'. If you wish to deviate and explore the area, ensure you retrace your steps and return to *The Salt Line.*

The Salt Line

8. In about a mile, pass a metal Salt Line Information Board, then almost immediately cross a road and continue ahead in the same direction. After another ¼ mile pass a sleeper, which has an interesting metal information plaque attached to it. The path goes under the motorway, and just over 100 yards further on and past what appears to have been the old station on the right, cross a road to return to the car park and your car.

'Heartbreak Hill'

See walk 21.

Thurlwood/Rode Heath

This settlement was once the site of more salt workings, but the canal side is now well landscaped and shows little sign of its industrial past.

The Salt Line

The Wheelock Branch of the Salt Line Railway opened in stages between 1852 and 1858. At first it was only a goods line, taking salt and products from the chemical industries in Cheshire to the Potteries, and returning with coal to power the machinery. When a passenger service was introduced in 1893, Trentham Gardens was a favourite destination. Passenger services ended in 1930 but goods were carried on this line until 1970.

Places you may wish to stop for refreshment

The Broughton Arms, Rode Heath: *01270 883203*
www.broughtonarmspub.co.uk *This is a Marstons Pub with a large menu. There is a patio where you can sit outside in the summer by the canal.*

WALK 23
Rode Heath to Hall Green via Hardings Wood Junction

Rode Heath – The Trent and Mersey Canal – Hardings Wood Junction/Kidsgrove – The Hall Green Branch of the Trent and Mersey Canal – Hall Green – Rode Heath

Starting point	**The Old Knutsford Road, off the A50 south of Rode Heath. Grid reference: 811567**
Length	**5½-6 miles**
Allow	**Approximately 2½ hours**
Map	**OS Explorer 268**
By car	**From the A50, about 250 yards south of its junction with the A533 Sandbach Road, (and 150 yards south of Cherry lane on the opposite side of the road) turn east onto the narrow Old Knutsford Road. Old Knutsford Road is between two areas of grass and is to your left if driving from Rode Heath and to your right if driving from Kidsgrove. Once you have turned, park on the left near some houses**

This is arguably one of the pleasantest walks on The Cheshire Canal Ring. There is a great variety of scenery and very little road walking. With 3¾ miles of towpath it is the longest canal stretch to be walked on the western side of The Cheshire Ring. However, the shorter distance between each end of the canal means the overall walk is not the longest. The canal section is especially interesting and includes the paired locks of *the Cheshire Flight or 'Heartbreak Hill'*, Hardings Wood Junction, Poole Aqueduct over the Trent and Mersey Canal, and some wide ranging views. The return is along undulating footpaths, across fields with sweeping vistas and through attractive wooded areas. This is all the more unexpected if a number of your previous walks have been across the seemingly flat Cheshire Plain.

The Walk

1. Walk back up to the A50. Turn right and cross the main road when it is safe to do so. After 150 yards turn left down Cherry Lane. Almost immediately you cross the canal bridge and then walk down to the left to join the towpath, Here you turn right. You will walk along the wide, well surfaced towpath for 2½ miles before joining The Hall Green Branch of The Trent and Mersey Canal at Hardings Wood Junction. Initially the water is to your left.

2. The canal bears right and after ¼ mile bends sharply to the left. Pass under the A50 and over Snapes Aqueduct before coming to a series of locks: nos. 52 to 47 near Church Lawton (Lawton Treble Locks and Church Locks). Later in the walk these are followed by locks 46 to 41 nearer Hardings Wood Junction. Together, these complete the flight known as *Heartbreak Hill,* which, starts near Wheelock and forms part of the climb up from The Cheshire Plain to the foothills of The Pennines.

3. The first locks you come to are the three Lawton paired locks (locks 52, 51 and 50). Note the overflow pool behind a wall by lock 52 and also note that one side of lock 51 has been filled in. Pass lock 50 then at the next bridge you will cross the canal. Immediately past the bridge is Lock 49 Hall's Lock. Note the view of Mow Cop in the distance. You will keep getting glimpses of it for the rest of the walk.

At Lock 49, Hall's Lock

Lawton Church

4. With the water on your right, you soon pass locks 48 and 47, after which the canal sweeps to the right and if you look carefully you can see Lawton Church behind the trees on the left. After walking under the busy A50 the

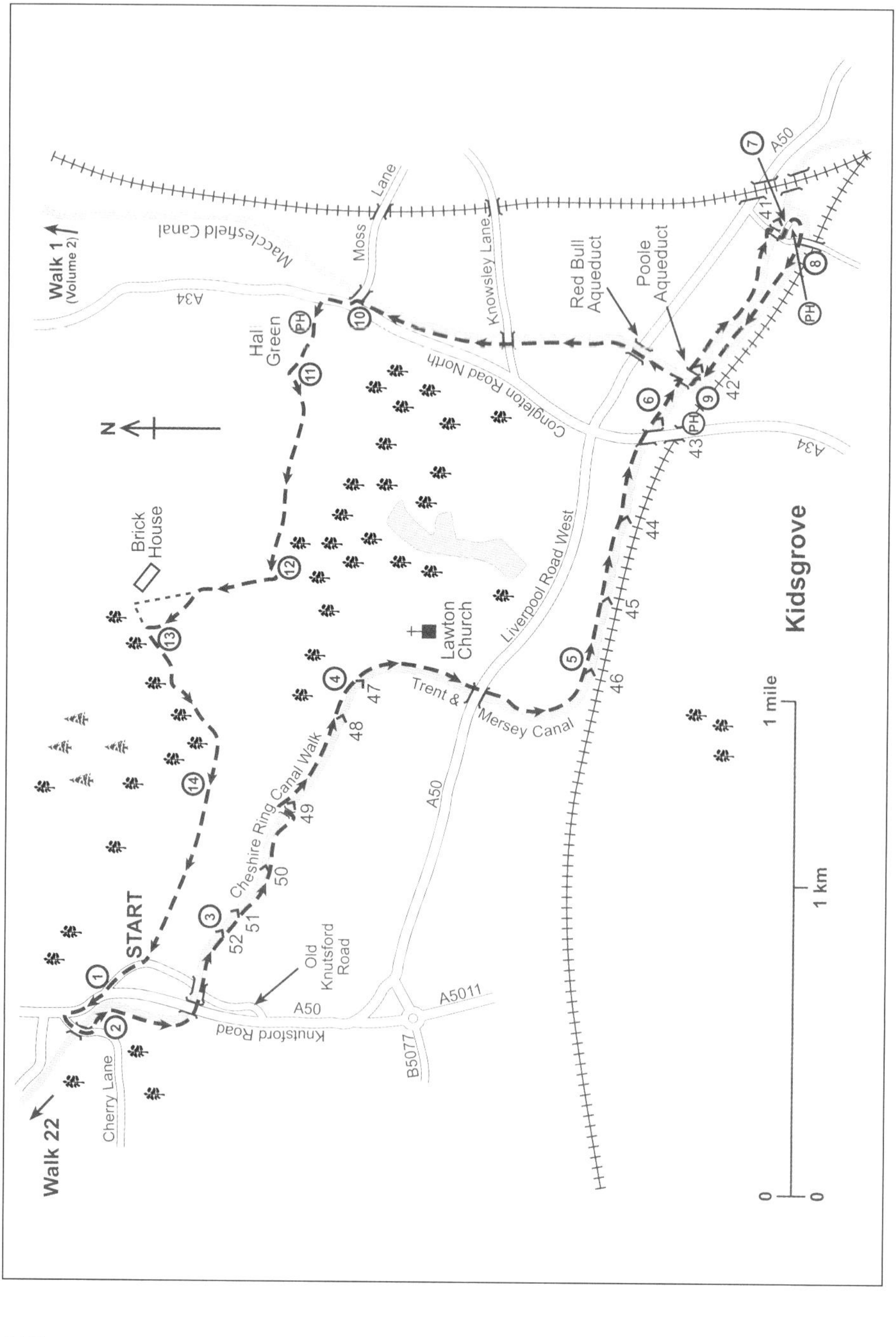
Walk 1 (Volume 2)
Macclesfield Canal
Moss Lane
Knowsley Lane
A34
Hall Green
PH
Red Bull Aqueduct
Poole Aqueduct
A50
Congleton Road North
N
Brick House
Liverpool Road West
Lawton Church
Kidsgrove
Trent & Mersey Canal
Cheshire Ring Canal Walk
A50
START
Old Knutsford Road
A50
A5011
Knutsford Road
B5077
Cherry Lane
Walk 22
1 mile
1 km
0
0

canal bears to the left. This and the next stretch of water up to the A34, is extremely pleasant. There is often a brownish hue to the water in this area which is the result of ironstone in the local rocks.

5. Climb 3 of the 4 *Red Bull Locks* (lock 46, 45 and 44) and whilst doing so note the trees shielding the railway line to the right and the old stone wall separating the towpath from fields sloping down to Lawton Woods and the A50 to the left. After Lock 44 pass some canal side services and two old canal side cranes, and walk under the A34 and past '*The Red Bull*', a Robinsons Pub on the opposite side of the canal. Lock 43 by the pub has been reduced to a single lock as the result of a road widening scheme.

6. Soon after the A34 you come to Poole Aqueduct which carries the *Hall Green Branch of the Trent and Mersey Canal.* This connects the Trent and Mersey mainline with the Macclesfield Canal at Hall Green. Don't be tempted to take a short cut up to the canal as you need to reach Hardings Wood Junction first if you want to say you have walked the whole of the Cheshire Ring! Pass lock 42 then walk along a wide, well tended stretch of towpath to reach Hardings Wood Road in just over ¼ mile. Here, with *The Canal Tavern* to your left, you turn right over the bridge to walk on the right hand side of the canal again. If you wish to visit *The Blue Bell Inn,* once you are over the bridge, walk ahead to the first road and turn left. Note that it is only open in the evening during the week.

7. Return to the towpath with the water now on your left. You immediately pass lock 41 and soon after this the towpath crosses a stone bridge at the junction of The Trent and Mersey Canal Mainline and the Hall Green Branch leading to the Macclesfield Canal. You may wish to go onto the bridge to look at the view and to see the signpost indicating that you are indeed on the Cheshire Ring. It tells you amongst other things that you have travelled 23 miles from Anderton along the Trent and Mersey Canal and that Manchester is 43 miles away along The Macclesfield Canal. However, to continue the walk, you must turn right just before reaching the bridge.

8. You are now on the short *Hall Green Branch of the Trent and Mersey Canal* which will take you to the Macclesfield Canal at Hall Green in just over a mile. You begin with the water on your left. The towpath is clear but narrow, so take care. The canal veers slightly to the right and soon you will notice a railway line to your left, followed by some well tended

permanent moorings, and if you are fortunate, you may see some interesting boats.

9. In slightly under ½ mile there is a sharp right hand bend, indicated to boaters by a warning sign, and just after the turn, cross over to the other side of the canal. Interestingly, the bridge you cross on (bridge 96) is numbered as the final bridge on the Macclesfield Canal even though you are not officially on that canal yet. Turn left off the bridge to walk across Poole Aqueduct which takes you over the main Trent and Mersey Canal and which you walked along earlier. Once over Poole Aqueduct you soon cross over the A50 on *Red Bull Aqueduct.* A little further on, walk under bridge 95 and just over a mile after Hardings Wood Junction as the canal enters a cutting, you leave the towpath at bridge 94 in Hall Green.

10. Turn left and almost immediately come to the A34. Turn right along the main road and you will see the large, thatched *Bleeding Wolf Inn* ahead on

Leaving the canal at bridge 94 of The Hall Green Branch

your left. Cross the road with care and turn down Bleeding Wolf Lane which is just before the pub - which is closed at present for refurbishment. Walk past a number of impressive gates on the left and then where the lane bears left between two posts towards what appear to be stables, continue ahead along a narrow path between two high hedges. At the end of this short stretch, and just over 250 yards after leaving the A34, there is a footpath sign ahead and also one to the left which takes you over a stile to the left of a part metal gate. Do not continue ahead but go over the left hand stile.

11. Once over the stile, walk ahead with a hedge on your right. Cross another stile and bear slightly right to walk diagonally across a second field. Follow the clear footpath signs, and at the end of this field go into a third field which you also cross diagonally. Here and for the rest of this section across the fields, enjoy the far reaching views all around you.

12. At the far corner of this field, dip down by some woodland. Go through a gate and over a stream, but then do not follow the left hand path which directs you ahead along the stream, but instead bear right through another gate and follow a path which leads you up diagonally right across another field to reach a track. Cross the track. A footpath sign directs you diagonally across the field ahead right, towards a wood. However, there is also a clear route leading directly ahead, and it's suggested that you walk ahead down here towards the wood, if you are able to do so.

13. When you reach the wood, turn left. The wood is now to your right and the field to your left. When you have walked about ¾ way across the large field, look out for a footpath sign on the right which takes you down a narrow path into the woods. Cross a stream then walk up the other side. Once out of the woodland, keep ahead left across a field, making sure you don't take a path on the far left that leads you down again towards the stream.

14. Continue in the same direction, passing through a number of fields on a well marked footpath. About half a mile after leaving the wood, you reach Old Knutsford Road. Cross the stile, descend two steps and turn right to return to your car.

The Cheshire Flight or 'Heartbreak Hill'

See walk 21.

Red Bull Locks, Red Bull Aqueduct

In 1775 Red Bull was a small hamlet and is now part of Kidsgrove. A number of structures in the area take its name, which is derived from the red colour of the ironstone in the locality

The Hall Green Branch of the Trent and Mersey Canal.

When The Macclesfield Canal was completed in 1831, the owners of The Trent and Mersey Canal saw it as a threat to their already established trade links with Manchester. In order to make things as difficult as possible for their new rival, they built a branch line from Hardings Wood Junction to Hall Green so the connection between the two canals would be well away from the already established Trent and Mersey main line. As a result two sets of stop locks, two lock keepers cottages and two stable blocks, one for each company, were built at Hall Green. Little of this is left but one stop lock is still in use, and can be seen just beyond bridge 94. Sometimes this short stretch from Hardings Wood Junction to Hall Green is mistakenly referred to as part of The Macclesfield Canal.

Places you may wish to stop for refreshment

The Red Bull, Kidsgrove: *01782 782600. This Robinsons pub can be recommended for a drink, and also for its food. It is pleasant to sit outside by the canal in the summer.*

The Canal Tavern, Hardings Wood Junction: *07533 101849*

The Blue Bell Inn, Hardings Wood: *01782 774052*

www.bluebellinnkidsgrove.com *This traditional drinkers' pub has been in the Good Beer Guide since 2000. During the week it is only open from 7.30pm.*

The Bleeding Wolf, Hall Green/Scholar Green: *01782 782272*

This large welcoming thatched Robinsons pub is a well known landmark and is worth visiting. Legend says that a local forester called Lawton saved King John from being killed by a wolf, and an inn was built on the spot the wolf died. Apparently, as a reward, Lawton was given an estate covering the land he could walk across from here in a week. As a result the word Lawton is in many of the local place names.

RECORD OF WALKS COMPLETED

Walk	Canal section	Length of walk	Date completed	Comments
1	Castlefield to Old Trafford	4½-5 miles		
2	Old Trafford to Stretford	5½ miles		
3	Stretford to Brooklands	6½ miles		
4	Brooklands to Seamons Moss	6 miles		
5	Seamons Moss to Little Bollington	4½-5 miles		
6	Little Bollington to Lymm	7 miles		
7	Lymm to Grappenhall	6½ miles		
8	Grappenhall to Stockton Heath	4½-5 miles		
9	Stockton Heath to Moore	7 miles		
10	Moore to Preston Brook	6½-7 miles		
11	Preston Brook to Lodge Lane	5½ miles		
12	Lodge Lane to south of Acton Bridge	5 miles		
13	South of Acton Bridge to Anderton	6½ miles		
14	Anderton to Marston	4½ miles		
15	Marston to Rudheath	4½ miles		
16	Rudheath to Whatcroft	5-5½ miles		
17	Whatcroft to The Big Lock, Middlewich	8½ miles		
18	The Big Lock, Middlewich to Tetton Bridge	6 miles		
19	Tetton Bridge to Elworth	5 miles		
20	Elworth to Wheelock	6½ miles		
21	Wheelock to Hassall Green	5 miles		
22	Hassall Green to Rode Heath	5 miles		
23	Rode Heath to Hall Green via Hardings Wood Junction	5½-6 miles		

Date of completion of the walks .... Congratulations!!